Best Flask API Development Practices

Don't Fear the Flask: Build APIs Like a Boss! Forge Your Backend with
Python's Microframework. Craft Clean, Secure, and Scalable APIs and more.

Katie Millie

Best Flask API Development Practices

Don't Fear the Flask: Build APIs Like a Boss! Forge Your Backend with Python's Microframework. Craft Clean, Secure, and Scalable APIs and more.

By

Katie Millie

Copyright notice

Copyright © 2024 Katie Millie. All rights reserved.

This work by Katie Millie is protected by copyright law, and any unauthorized reproduction, distribution, or transmission—whether electronic, mechanical, photocopying, recording, or otherwise—is strictly prohibited without the prior written consent of the author. Only brief quotations used in critical reviews or specific noncommercial purposes allowed by copyright law are exempt from this restriction. Any infringement will lead to legal action.

Katie Millie puts immense effort and creativity into producing her unique and engaging content. Protecting this intellectual property is vital to maintaining the integrity and originality of her work. If you wish to use any part of this content for educational, scholarly, or other purposes beyond what copyright law permits, please seek written permission from the author. By respecting these guidelines, you contribute to a culture that values and supports creativity, enabling Katie Millie to continue offering her inspiring work to the world. Thank you for your understanding and cooperation.

Table of Contents

INTRODUCTION
Chapter 1
    Why Flask for APIs? The Power of Flexibility
        The Core Concepts: Routes, Views, and Templates (Oh My!)
            Setting Up Your Development Environment for Flask API Development
            Hello, World! Your First Flask API
Chapter 2
    Structuring for Success: Organizing Your Flask Application
        Blueprints: Modularizing Your API for Maintainability
            Dependency Injection: Keeping Your Code Clean and Organized
                Configuration Management: Keeping Secrets Secret
Chapter 3
    RESTful Design Principles: Building a Consistent and Predictable API
        HTTP Methods: Verbs that Make Your API Dance (GET, POST, PUT, DELETE)
            Resource-Oriented Design: Structuring Endpoints Around Your Data
                Versioning Your API: Ensuring Smooth Transitions and Backward Compatibility
Chapter 4

Working with Data: From Simple Variables to Databases with SQLAlchemy

Data Validation: Ensuring Your API Receives Clean Data

Serialization: Transforming Data for Seamless Consumption by Clients

Common Data Formats: JSON, XML, and Beyond

Chapter 5

Understanding Authentication Mechanisms: Basic, Token-Based, and More

Implementing Authentication with Flask Extensions

Session Management: Keeping Users Logged In

Chapter 6

Role-Based Access Control (RBAC): Granular Control Over User Permissions

Protecting Specific Resources and Endpoints

Best Practices for Secure Authorization

Chapter 7

Unit Testing: Isolating and Validating Individual Components

Integration Testing: Ensuring Different Parts of Your API Work Together Seamlessly

Test-Driven Development (TDD): A Proactive Approach to Building Robust APIs

Popular Testing Frameworks for Flask: Unittest, pytest, and More

Chapter 8

Setting Up a Local Development Server for Testing

and Iteration
- Deployment Options: Cloud Platforms like Heroku and AWS
  - Configuration Management for Production Environments
    - Monitoring and Logging: Keeping an Eye on Your Deployed API

Chapter 9
- Clean Coding Principles: Writing Code You (and Others) Can Love
  - Code Formatting and Linting: Enforcing Consistency and Style
    - Documentation: The User Manual for Your API

Chapter 10
- Marshmallow: Effortless Data Serialization and Validation
  - Other Useful Extensions for Common Tasks

Conclusion
- Appendix
  - Glossary of terms
    - Common Flask API Development Pitfalls (and How to Avoid Them!)

INTRODUCTION

Forge Your Flask: Master the Art of API Development

Have you ever dreamt of building the backend muscle for the next killer app? The one that seamlessly connects users, data, and functionality with the power of APIs? Well, fret no more, fellow Pythonista! Because within these pages lies the key to unlocking your Flask API development mastery.

This isn't your average, dry technical manual. We're diving headfirst into the exciting world of crafting clean, robust, and secure APIs with Flask, the Python microframework that's become a developer darling. But why Flask? Because Flask empowers you to be the architect, not a slave to a rigid framework. It grants you the freedom to design, build, and scale your API with elegance and efficiency.

But fear not, fledgling developer! We understand the initial hurdles. You might be grappling with questions like:

- How do I structure my API for optimal clarity and maintainability?
- What are the secret ingredients for crafting powerful and versatile endpoints?

- How do I ensure my API is battle-tested and secure from prying eyes?
- And the ultimate question: How do I write clean, maintainable code that future me (or your teammates) will love?

This book is your roadmap to conquering these challenges and more. We'll hold your hand (virtually, of course) as you:

- **Craft a Flawless Foundation:** Learn the core principles of Flask API development, from structuring your application to wielding the power of Blueprints for modularity.
- **Sculpt Meaningful Endpoints:** Master the art of designing intuitive and RESTful endpoints that make perfect sense to both you and anyone using your API.
- **Embrace the Power of Data:** Explore effective data handling techniques, from working with databases like SQLAlchemy to crafting elegant data validation and serialization.
- **Security: Your API's Shield:** Delve into the essential security measures to protect your API from unauthorized access and vulnerabilities. Learn about authentication, authorization, and best practices to keep your data safe.
- **Testing: Building Confidence:** Discover the importance of unit and integration testing, and equip yourself with the tools to write robust tests that ensure your API functions flawlessly.

- **Deployment: Sharing Your Creation:** Learn the secrets of deploying your API to the real world, whether on a local server or a cloud platform.

But this book isn't just about technical prowess. We'll also explore the art of clean coding, design patterns that promote maintainability, and the importance of clear documentation – because even the most brilliant code needs a user manual!

We'll unveil the power of tools like Flask-RESTful and Marshmallow to streamline your development process. We'll even sprinkle in some real-world examples to show you how these concepts come to life.

So, are you ready to unleash the full potential of Flask for API development? Are you eager to craft APIs that are not just functional, but elegant, secure, and a joy to work with? Then turn the page and let's embark on this exciting journey together!

Chapter 1

Why Flask for APIs? The Power of Flexibility

When it comes to building APIs, Flask stands out for its flexibility, simplicity, and scalability. Flask, a lightweight and modular micro-framework for Python, empowers developers to craft robust APIs with ease. Let's delve into why Flask is the preferred choice for API development, exploring its key features and best practices along the way.

1. Simplicity and Minimalism

Flask's minimalist design makes it incredibly simple to get started with API development. With Flask, you only get what you need, keeping your codebase clean and uncluttered. Let's kick off with a basic example:

```python
from flask import Flask

app = Flask(__name__)

@app.route('/api/v1/hello')
def hello():
    return 'Hello, World!'
```

```
if __name__ == '__main__':
    app.run(debug=True)
```

In this example, we create a Flask application and define a route `/api/v1/hello` that returns a simple greeting. Running this code launches a development server, ready to handle API requests.

2. Flexibility in URL Routing

Flask offers flexible URL routing, allowing developers to define routes for API endpoints effortlessly. You can specify dynamic parameters in URLs, making your API more versatile. Consider this example:

```python
@app.route('/api/v1/user/<int:user_id>')
def get_user(user_id):
    # Retrieve user information based on user_id
    return jsonify({'user_id': user_id, 'name': 'John Doe'})
```

Here, the route `/api/v1/user/<int:user_id>` captures an integer parameter `user_id`, enabling the retrieval of user information based on the provided ID.

3. Lightweight and Extensible

Flask's lightweight nature doesn't compromise extensibility. Developers can easily integrate additional functionality using Flask extensions. These extensions cover a wide range of features such as authentication, database integration, and caching. Let's incorporate Flask-RESTful, an extension for building REST APIs:

```python
from flask import Flask
from flask_restful import Resource, Api

app = Flask(__name__)
api = Api(app)

class HelloWorld(Resource):
    def get(self):
        return {'hello': 'world'}

api.add_resource(HelloWorld, '/api/v1/hello')

if __name__ == '__main__':
    app.run(debug=True)
```

In this example, we enhance our API with Flask-RESTful to create a RESTful endpoint for greeting.

4. JSON Support

Flask simplifies handling JSON data, a fundamental aspect of modern API development. It seamlessly serializes and deserializes JSON objects, streamlining data exchange between clients and servers. Take a look at how easy it is to handle JSON requests:

```python
from flask import Flask, jsonify, request

app = Flask(__name__)

@app.route('/api/v1/users', methods=['POST'])
def create_user():
    user_data = request.get_json()
    # Process user_data
    return jsonify({'message': 'User created successfully'})

if __name__ == '__main__':
    app.run(debug=True)
```

Here, we define an endpoint `/api/v1/users` to handle POST requests for creating users. The `request.get_json()` method extracts JSON data from the request, allowing seamless integration with client applications.

5. Testing Made Easy

Flask simplifies the testing process, enabling developers to write comprehensive test suites effortlessly. The built-in testing framework and support for third-party testing libraries facilitate unit testing, integration testing, and end-to-end testing. Let's write a simple test case using Flask's testing client:

```python
import unittest
from app import app

class TestApp(unittest.TestCase):
    def setUp(self):
        self.app = app.test_client()

    def test_hello_endpoint(self):
        response = self.app.get('/api/v1/hello')
        self.assertEqual(response.status_code, 200)
        self.assertEqual(response.data.decode(), '{"hello":"world"}')

if __name__ == '__main__':
    unittest.main()
```

In this example, we test the `/api/v1/hello` endpoint to ensure it returns the expected JSON response.

Best Practices for Flask API Development:

1. Organize Your Code: Follow a modular structure to keep your code organized and maintainable. Separate concerns into different modules or packages.

2. Use Blueprints: Utilize Flask Blueprints to partition your application into reusable components, promoting scalability and code reusability.

3. Implement Error Handling: Handle errors gracefully by providing meaningful error messages and appropriate HTTP status codes.

4. Security Measures: Implement security best practices such as input validation, authentication, and authorization to protect your API from common vulnerabilities.

5. Versioning: Incorporate versioning in your API endpoints to ensure backward compatibility and smooth transitions between API versions.

6. Documentation: Document your API thoroughly using tools like Swagger or Flask-RESTPlus to improve developer experience and promote adoption.

7. Performance Optimization: Optimize performance by employing caching mechanisms, optimizing database queries, and implementing asynchronous processing where applicable.

lask offers unparalleled flexibility and simplicity for API development. Its minimalist design, coupled with a rich ecosystem of extensions, empowers developers to build robust and scalable APIs efficiently. By adhering to best practices, you can leverage Flask's full potential and deliver exceptional API experiences to your users.

The Core Concepts: Routes, Views, and Templates (Oh My!)

In Flask development, mastering the core concepts of routes, views, and templates is essential for building powerful and maintainable web applications. These elements form the backbone of Flask applications, facilitating URL routing, request handling, and rendering dynamic content. Let's delve into each of these concepts, exploring best practices and code examples along the way.

1. Routes: Mapping URLs to Functions

Routes define the mapping between URLs and corresponding functions in your Flask application. They determine how incoming requests are processed and which functions are invoked to generate responses. Here's a basic example of defining routes in Flask:

```python
from flask import Flask

app = Flask(__name__)

@app.route('/')
def index():
    return 'Welcome to Flask!'

@app.route('/about')
def about():
    return 'About Flask'

if __name__ == '__main__':
    app.run(debug=True)
```

In this example, we define two routes: `/` for the index page and `/about` for an about page. Each route is associated with a function that returns the content to be displayed when the corresponding URL is accessed.

2. Views: Request Handling and Business Logic

Views are Python functions responsible for handling incoming requests and executing the necessary business logic. They process data, interact with databases, and orchestrate the generation of responses. Let's enhance our previous example by incorporating views with more complex logic:

```python
from flask import Flask, render_template

app = Flask(__name__)

@app.route('/')
def index():
    return render_template('index.html', title='Home', content='Welcome to Flask!')

@app.route('/about')
def about():
    return render_template('about.html', title='About', content='About Flask')

if __name__ == '__main__':
```

```
app.run(debug=True)
```

In this updated example, we use the `render_template` function to render HTML templates for the index and about pages. These templates allow for more dynamic content generation and separation of concerns between presentation and logic.

3. Templates: Dynamic Content Rendering

Templates are HTML files containing placeholders for dynamic content generated by Flask views. They enable the separation of concerns between the presentation layer and application logic, facilitating code maintainability and reusability. Let's create template files for our index and about pages:

index.html:

```html
<!DOCTYPE html>
<html lang="en">
<head>
    <meta charset="UTF-8">
    <meta name="viewport" content="width=device-width, initial-scale=1.0">
    <title>{{ title }}</title>
```

```
  </head>
  <body>
      <h1>{{ content }}</h1>
  </body>
</html>
```

about.html:

```html
<!DOCTYPE html>
<html lang="en">
<head>
    <meta charset="UTF-8">
    <meta name="viewport" content="width=device-width, initial-scale=1.0">
    <title>{{ title }}</title>
</head>
<body>
    <h1>{{ content }}</h1>
</body>
</html>
```

These template files use Jinja2 syntax to insert dynamic content provided by Flask views. The `{{ title }}` and `{{ content }}` placeholders are replaced with actual values when the templates are rendered.

Best Practices for Routes, Views, and Templates:

1. Keep Routes Concise: Define clear and concise routes that reflect the structure of your application. Avoid overly complex URLs and adhere to RESTful principles where applicable.

2. Separation of Concerns: Separate business logic from presentation by placing logic in views and rendering dynamic content in templates. This promotes code maintainability and facilitates collaboration between developers.

3. Use Template Inheritance: Leverage template inheritance to create reusable layouts and avoid duplication of code across multiple pages. Define a base template that contains common elements and extends it in child templates as needed.

4. Parameterized URLs: Utilize parameterized URLs to handle dynamic data in routes, improving flexibility and readability. Parameterized routes allow for variable parts in URLs, enabling dynamic content generation based on user input or database queries.

5. Error Handling: Implement error handling in routes to gracefully manage unexpected scenarios and provide meaningful error messages to users. Flask provides mechanisms for handling common HTTP errors like 404 (Not Found) and 500 (Internal Server Error).

6. Static Files: Serve static files (e.g., CSS, JavaScript, images) efficiently by utilizing Flask's built-in static file handling capabilities. Organize static files in a dedicated directory and reference them using the `url_for` function to ensure proper URL generation.

7. Testing Routes and Views: Write comprehensive test cases to ensure the correctness and reliability of routes and views. Use Flask's testing framework or third-party libraries like pytest to automate testing and verify the behavior of your application under different scenarios.

By mastering routes, views, and templates, you'll be well-equipped to develop robust and scalable Flask applications. These core concepts form the foundation of Flask development, empowering you to create dynamic web applications with ease and elegance. Embrace best practices and leverage the flexibility of Flask to build exceptional web experiences for your users.

Setting Up Your Development Environment for Flask API Development

Creating a conducive development environment is crucial for productive Flask API development. A well-configured environment ensures smooth workflow, efficient debugging, and seamless collaboration. Let's explore the essential steps and best practices for setting up your Flask development environment.

1. Python Installation and Virtual Environments

Python is the backbone of Flask development, so ensure you have Python installed on your system. It's recommended to use Python 3.x, preferably the latest stable version.

Next, set up a virtual environment to isolate your project dependencies. Virtual environments prevent conflicts between different projects and facilitate dependency management. Here's how to create and activate a virtual environment:

```bash
# Create a virtual environment
python3 -m venv myprojectenv

# Activate the virtual environment
source myprojectenv/bin/activate    # On Unix/macOS
myprojectenv\Scripts\activate       # On Windows
```

2. Installing Flask and Dependencies

Once inside your virtual environment, install Flask and any additional dependencies your project requires. It's best to maintain a `requirements.txt` file listing all dependencies for easy installation. Here's how to install Flask:

```bash
pip install Flask
```

You can also install specific versions of Flask or other packages by specifying them in your `requirements.txt` file and installing them using:

```bash
pip install -r requirements.txt
```

3. Project Structure

A well-organized project structure enhances code readability, maintainability, and scalability. Follow a consistent structure to keep your Flask projects organized. Here's a suggested project structure:

```
myproject/
├── app/
│   ├── __init__.py
│   ├── routes.py
│   ├── models.py
│   ├── templates/
│   └── static/
│
├── tests/
│   └── test_routes.py
│
├── config.py
├── requirements.txt
└── run.py
```

- **app/:** Contains your application's code.

- **__init__.py:** Initializes the Flask application.

- **routes.py:** Defines route mappings and view functions.

- **models.py:** Contains data models (if using a database).

- **templates/:** Directory for HTML templates.

- **static/:** Directory for static files (CSS, JavaScript, images).

- **tests/:** Directory for test files.

- **config.py:** Configuration settings for the application.

- **requirements.txt:** List of project dependencies.

- **run.py:** Entry point to run the Flask application.

4. Configuration Management

Separate configuration settings from your application code to enable flexibility and maintainability. Flask provides a built-in configuration mechanism that allows you to define configuration variables in a separate file. Here's an example of a `config.py` file:

```python
class Config:
    DEBUG = True
    SECRET_KEY = 'your_secret_key_here'
    SQLALCHEMY_DATABASE_URI = 'sqlite:///mydatabase.db'
```

```

You can then load configuration settings in your Flask application using:

```python
from flask import Flask

app = Flask(__name__)
app.config.from_object('config.Config')
```

5. Database Integration

If your Flask API requires database functionality, integrate a database into your project. SQLAlchemy is a popular choice for database ORM in Flask applications. Install SQLAlchemy and the database driver you'll be using:

```bash
pip install SQLAlchemy
pip install psycopg2     # for PostgreSQL
pip install pymysql      # for MySQL
pip install sqlite3      # for SQLite (included in Python standard library)
```
```

Configure the database URI in your `config.py` file as shown in the previous step.

6. Version Control with Git

Version control is indispensable for collaborative development and code management. Initialize a Git repository in your project directory:

```bash
git init
```

Commit your initial project files and create a `.gitignore` file to exclude unnecessary files from version control (e.g., virtual environment files, database files).

7. Development Server and Debugging

Flask provides a built-in development server for testing and debugging your application locally. Run your Flask application using the `run.py` script:

```python
from app import app

if __name__ == '__main__':
    app.run(debug=True)
```

```

Enable debug mode (`debug=True`) to automatically reload the server when code changes are detected and to display detailed error messages in the browser.

## 8. Testing Your Application

Write comprehensive test suites to verify the functionality of your Flask API. Use testing frameworks like unittest or pytest to automate testing and ensure code reliability. Place your test files in the `tests/` directory and execute them using:

```bash
python -m unittest discover -s tests
```

9. Continuous Integration (CI)

Integrate Continuous Integration (CI) into your development workflow to automate testing and deployment processes. Platforms like GitHub Actions, Travis CI, or GitLab CI can be used to set up CI pipelines that run tests whenever code changes are pushed to the repository.
```

By following these best practices, you'll establish a robust development environment for Flask API development. Organize your project structure, manage dependencies efficiently, and leverage tools like Git and CI to streamline your workflow. With a well-configured environment in place, you'll be equipped to build and deploy scalable Flask APIs with confidence.

Hello, World! Your First Flask API

Embarking on your Flask API journey begins with a simple "Hello, World!" application. In this guide, we'll walk through the process of creating your first Flask API, adhering to best practices every step of the way. Let's dive in!

1. Setting Up Your Project

Start by setting up your project directory and creating a virtual environment to isolate dependencies. Here's how you can do it:

```bash
# Create a new directory for your project
mkdir hello_flask_api
cd hello_flask_api

# Create a virtual environment
```

```
python3 -m venv venv

# Activate the virtual environment
source venv/bin/activate    # On Unix/macOS
venv\Scripts\activate       # On Windows
```

2. Installing Flask

With your virtual environment activated, install Flask using pip:

```bash
pip install Flask
```

Flask will be our primary tool for building the API.

3. Creating Your Flask App

Now, let's create a basic Flask application. Create a file named `app.py` in your project directory and add the following code:

```python
from flask import Flask

app = Flask(__name__)
```

```
@app.route('/')
def hello_world():
    return 'Hello, World!'

if __name__ == '__main__':
    app.run(debug=True)
```

In this code:

- We import the `Flask` class from the `flask` module.

- We create an instance of the `Flask` class and assign it to the `app` variable.

- We define a route using the `@app.route()` decorator. This route maps the URL `/` to the `hello_world()` function.

- The `hello_world()` function returns the string "Hello, World!".

- Finally, we use `app.run()` to start the development server.

4. Running Your Flask App

To run your Flask application, execute the following command in your terminal:

```bash
python app.py
```

You should see output indicating that the development server is running. Open your web browser and navigate to `http://127.0.0.1:5000/`. You should see the "Hello, World!" message displayed in the browser.

5. Enhancing Your API

Let's enhance our "Hello, World!" API by adding a few more routes and returning JSON responses. Update your `app.py` file as follows:

```python
from flask import Flask, jsonify

app = Flask(__name__)

@app.route('/')
def hello_world():
    return 'Hello, World!'
```

```
@app.route('/api/v1/hello')
def hello_api():
    return jsonify({'message': 'Hello, API!'})

@app.route('/api/v1/greet/<string:name>')
def greet(name):
    return jsonify({'message': f'Hello, {name}!'})

if __name__ == '__main__':
    app.run(debug=True)
```
```

In this updated code:

- We define two new routes: `/api/v1/hello` and `/api/v1/greet/<string:name>`.

- The `/api/v1/hello` route returns a JSON response with the message "Hello, API!".

- The `/api/v1/greet/<string:name>` route takes a name parameter and returns a personalized greeting in JSON format.

## 6. Testing Your API

Testing is an integral part of API development. Let's write a simple test script to verify the functionality of our
```

API. Create a file named `test_api.py` in your project directory with the following content:

```python
import requests

def test_hello_api():
    response = requests.get('http://127.0.0.1:5000/api/v1/hello')
    assert response.status_code == 200
    assert response.json() == {'message': 'Hello, API!'}

def test_greet_api():
    response = requests.get('http://127.0.0.1:5000/api/v1/greet/John')
    assert response.status_code == 200
    assert response.json() == {'message': 'Hello, John!'}
```

This test script sends HTTP requests to our API endpoints and verifies that the responses match the expected JSON format.

To run the tests, execute the following command in your terminal:

```bash
pytest test_api.py
```

```

If everything is set up correctly, you should see output indicating that both tests have passed.

Congratulations! You've successfully built and tested your first Flask API. This "Hello, World!" example serves as a foundation for more complex API development projects. As you continue your Flask journey, explore additional features such as request handling, database integration, authentication, and deployment. By following best practices and experimenting with Flask's capabilities, you'll unlock endless possibilities for building powerful and scalable APIs. Keep coding, and happy Flasking!
```

Chapter 2

Structuring for Success: Organizing Your Flask Application

Flask is a lightweight and flexible web framework for Python, making it an excellent choice for developing APIs. Properly structuring a Flask application is crucial for maintaining scalability, readability, and ease of maintenance. This guide outlines best practices for organizing a Flask application, complete with code examples.

1. Project Layout

A well-structured Flask project typically follows a layout that separates concerns and makes the codebase manageable. Here is a common directory structure for a Flask application:

```
/your_flask_app
│
├── app/
│   ├── __init__.py
│   ├── routes/
│   │   ├── __init__.py
│   │   ├── user_routes.py
```

```
│   │       └── product_routes.py
│   ├── models.py
│   ├── schemas.py
│   ├── extensions.py
│   ├── config.py
│   └── utils.py
│
├── tests/
│   ├── __init__.py
│   ├── test_users.py
│   └── test_products.py
│
├── migrations/
│   └── versions/
│
├── instance/
│   └── config.py
│
├── .env
├── requirements.txt
├── run.py
└── README.md
```

2. Application Factory Pattern

Using the application factory pattern allows you to create multiple instances of the app with different configurations, which is useful for testing.

`app/__init__.py`:

```python
from flask import Flask
from app.extensions import db, migrate
from app.config import Config

def create_app(config_class=Config):
    app = Flask(__name__)
    app.config.from_object(config_class)

    db.init_app(app)
    migrate.init_app(app, db)

    from app.routes import user_routes, product_routes
    app.register_blueprint(user_routes.bp)
    app.register_blueprint(product_routes.bp)

    return app
```

`app/config.py`:

```python
```

```python
class Config:
    SECRET_KEY = 'your_secret_key'
    SQLALCHEMY_DATABASE_URI = 'sqlite:///site.db'
    SQLALCHEMY_TRACK_MODIFICATIONS = False
```

`app/extensions.py`:

```python
from flask_sqlalchemy import SQLAlchemy
from flask_migrate import Migrate

db = SQLAlchemy()
migrate = Migrate()
```

3. Blueprints for Modularization

Using Blueprints, you can organize your application into distinct modules.

`app/routes/user_routes.py`:

```python
from flask import Blueprint, jsonify, request
from app.models import User
```

```python
from app.schemas import user_schema, users_schema
from app.extensions import db

bp = Blueprint('users', __name__)

@bp.route('/users', methods=['GET'])
def get_users():
    users = User.query.all()
    return users_schema.jsonify(users)

@bp.route('/users/<int:id>', methods=['GET'])
def get_user(id):
    user = User.query.get_or_404(id)
    return user_schema.jsonify(user)

@bp.route('/users', methods=['POST'])
def create_user():
    data = request.get_json()
    new_user = User(name=data['name'], email=data['email'])
    db.session.add(new_user)
    db.session.commit()
    return user_schema.jsonify(new_user), 201
```

`app/routes/product_routes.py`:

```python
```

```python
from flask import Blueprint, jsonify, request
from app.models import Product
from app.schemas import product_schema, products_schema
from app.extensions import db

bp = Blueprint('products', __name__)

@bp.route('/products', methods=['GET'])
def get_products():
    products = Product.query.all()
    return products_schema.jsonify(products)

@bp.route('/products/<int:id>', methods=['GET'])
def get_product(id):
    product = Product.query.get_or_404(id)
    return product_schema.jsonify(product)

@bp.route('/products', methods=['POST'])
def create_product():
    data = request.get_json()
    new_product = Product(name=data['name'], price=data['price'])
    db.session.add(new_product)
    db.session.commit()
    return product_schema.jsonify(new_product), 201
```

4. Models

Models define the structure of the database and are typically located in a single file.

`app/models.py`:

```python
from app.extensions import db

class User(db.Model):
    id = db.Column(db.Integer, primary_key=True)
    name = db.Column(db.String(50), nullable=False)
    email = db.Column(db.String(120), unique=True, nullable=False)

class Product(db.Model):
    id = db.Column(db.Integer, primary_key=True)
    name = db.Column(db.String(100), nullable=False)
    price = db.Column(db.Float, nullable=False)
```

5. Schemas for Serialization

Using schemas helps in serializing and deserializing models.

`app/schemas.py`:

```python
from flask_marshmallow import Marshmallow
from app.models import User, Product

ma = Marshmallow()

class UserSchema(ma.SQLAlchemyAutoSchema):
    class Meta:
        model = User

user_schema = UserSchema()
users_schema = UserSchema(many=True)

class ProductSchema(ma.SQLAlchemyAutoSchema):
    class Meta:
        model = Product

product_schema = ProductSchema()
products_schema = ProductSchema(many=True)
```

6. Utility Functions

Utility functions can be stored in a separate file to keep your code organized.

`app/utils.py`:

```python
def calculate_discount(price, discount):
    return price * (1 - discount / 100)
```

7. Configuration Management

Separate configuration files help manage different environments such as development, testing, and production.

`instance/config.py`:

```python
class DevelopmentConfig:
    DEBUG = True
    SQLALCHEMY_DATABASE_URI = 'sqlite:///dev.db'

class TestingConfig:
    TESTING = True
    SQLALCHEMY_DATABASE_URI = 'sqlite:///test.db'

class ProductionConfig:
    SQLALCHEMY_DATABASE_URI = 'sqlite:///prod.db'
```

```

## 8. Running the Application

A simple script to run your Flask application.

`run.py`:

```python
from app import create_app

app = create_app()

if __name__ == '__main__':
    app.run(debug=True)
```

9. Testing

Tests should be organized in a separate directory and should cover various aspects of your application.

`tests/test_users.py`:

```python
import unittest
from app import create_app, db
from app.models import User

```python
class UserTestCase(unittest.TestCase):
    def setUp(self):
        self.app = create_app('TestingConfig')
        self.app_context = self.app.app_context()
        self.app_context.push()
        db.create_all()

    def tearDown(self):
        db.session.remove()
        db.drop_all()
        self.app_context.pop()

    def test_user_creation(self):
        user = User(name='Test User', email='test@example.com')
        db.session.add(user)
        db.session.commit()
        self.assertIsNotNone(User.query.get(1))

if __name__ == '__main__':
    unittest.main()
```
```

## 10. Environment Variables

Using environment variables for sensitive information like secret keys and database URIs.
```

`.env`:

```
SECRET_KEY=your_secret_key
DATABASE_URL=sqlite:///site.db
```

Organizing your Flask application correctly is vital for maintaining a scalable, maintainable, and efficient codebase. By following the best practices outlined in this guide, you can ensure that your Flask application is well-structured and ready for growth. The use of the application factory pattern, Blueprints, proper configuration management, and thorough testing are key components of a successful Flask application.

Regularly reviewing and refactoring your code, as well as staying updated with the latest Flask best practices and updates, will help keep your application robust and efficient.

Blueprints: Modularizing Your API for Maintainability

As your Flask API grows in complexity, maintaining a clean and organized codebase becomes increasingly important. Flask Blueprints provide a solution to this challenge by enabling modularization of your API into smaller, reusable components. In this guide, we'll explore how to leverage Flask Blueprints to enhance the maintainability of your API, following best practices along the way.

1. Understanding Flask Blueprints

Flask Blueprints are a way to organize related views, routes, and templates into separate modules within your Flask application. They allow you to encapsulate functionality into distinct units, making your codebase more modular and easier to manage. Blueprints promote code reuse, facilitate collaboration between developers, and enable better organization of larger projects.

2. Creating a Blueprint

Let's start by creating a simple Flask Blueprint for managing user-related functionality. Create a new directory named `users` inside your `app` directory. Within the `users` directory, create a file named `routes.py` and add the following code:

```python
from flask import Blueprint, jsonify

users_bp = Blueprint('users', __name__)
```

```
@users_bp.route('/users', methods=['GET'])
def get_users():
    # Placeholder logic to retrieve users
    users = [{'id': 1, 'username': 'john'}, {'id': 2, 'username': 'jane'}]
    return jsonify(users)
```

In this code:

- We import the `Blueprint` class from Flask.

- We create a new Blueprint named `users_bp` with the name 'users'.

- We define a route `/users` within the Blueprint to retrieve a list of users.

- The `get_users()` function returns a JSON response containing a list of dummy user data.

3. Registering the Blueprint

Next, we need to register the Blueprint with our Flask application. Open your `app/__init__.py` file and update it as follows:

```python
from flask import Flask
from .users.routes import users_bp

def create_app():
    app = Flask(__name__)

    # Register the users Blueprint
    app.register_blueprint(users_bp, url_prefix='/api/v1')

    return app
```

In this code:

- We import the `users_bp` Blueprint from the `users.routes` module.

- We define a factory function `create_app()` to create our Flask application.

- We register the `users_bp` Blueprint with the application using the `app.register_blueprint()` method. We also specify a URL prefix `/api/v1` for all routes defined within the Blueprint.

4. Organizing Your Project Structure

To maintain a clean project structure, it's important to organize your Blueprints, views, and other components properly. Here's how you can structure your Flask project with Blueprints:

```
myproject/
│
├── app/
│   ├── __init__.py
│   ├── users/
│   │   ├── __init__.py
│   │   └── routes.py
│   ├── posts/
│   │   ├── __init__.py
│   │   └── routes.py
│   └── templates/
│
├── tests/
│
├── config.py
├── requirements.txt
└── run.py
```

Each Blueprint (e.g., `users`, `posts`) has its own directory containing a `routes.py` file with route definitions. This structure promotes separation of concerns and makes it easy to add, remove, or modify functionality within each module.

5. Testing Your Blueprint

Testing is crucial to ensure the correctness and reliability of your Blueprint. Let's write a simple test case to verify the behavior of the `/users` route. Create a file named `test_users.py` inside the `tests` directory with the following content:

```python
import pytest
from app import create_app

@pytest.fixture
def app():
    app = create_app()
    yield app

@pytest.fixture
def client(app):
    return app.test_client()

def test_get_users(client):
    response = client.get('/api/v1/users')
    assert response.status_code == 200
```

```
    assert response.json == [{'id': 1, 'username': 'john'},
{'id': 2, 'username': 'jane'}]
```

This test script uses pytest fixtures to set up the Flask application and client, then sends a GET request to the `/api/v1/users` route and verifies the response.

Flask Blueprints provide a powerful mechanism for organizing and modularizing your API, enhancing maintainability and scalability. By encapsulating related functionality into separate modules, you can keep your codebase clean and manageable, promote code reuse, and facilitate collaboration among developers. Incorporate Blueprints into your Flask projects following the best practices outlined in this guide, and you'll be well-equipped to build robust and maintainable APIs. Happy Flasking!

Dependency Injection: Keeping Your Code Clean and Organized

In Flask API development, maintaining clean and organized code is essential for scalability, maintainability, and ease of collaboration. Dependency injection is a design pattern that promotes loose coupling between components, making your code more modular and easier to test. In this guide, we'll explore how to leverage dependency injection in your Flask API using best practices and code examples.

1. Understanding Dependency Injection

Dependency injection is a software design pattern that enables components to be loosely coupled by injecting their dependencies rather than creating them internally. This allows for greater flexibility, as components can be easily replaced or modified without affecting the rest of the system. In the context of Flask API development, dependency injection can be used to inject services, configurations, or other dependencies into route handlers, views, or other components.

2. Using Dependency Injection in Flask

Let's start by looking at a simple example of dependency injection in Flask. Suppose we have a service class `UserService` responsible for managing user-related functionality. We want to inject an instance of this service into our route handlers. Here's how we can do it:

```python
from flask import Flask, jsonify
from flask_injector import FlaskInjector
from injector import inject
from services import UserService
```

```python
app = Flask(__name__)

@app.route('/users')
@inject
def get_users(user_service: UserService):
    users = user_service.get_all_users()
    return jsonify(users)

def configure(binder):
    binder.bind(UserService, to=UserService())

FlaskInjector(app=app, modules=[configure])

if __name__ == '__main__':
    app.run(debug=True)
```

In this code:

- We define a route `/users` that calls the `get_users()` function to retrieve a list of users.

- The `get_users()` function takes an instance of `UserService` as an argument. This instance is injected using the `@inject` decorator from the `injector` package.

- We define a `configure()` function that binds the `UserService` class to an instance of `UserService`. This function is passed to `FlaskInjector` to configure dependency injection for our Flask application.

3. Managing Configuration with Dependency Injection

Dependency injection can also be used to inject configuration settings into your Flask application. This allows you to decouple configuration from your code, making it easier to manage and test different configurations. Here's an example of injecting configuration using Flask-Injector and the `injector` package:

```python
from flask import Flask, jsonify
from flask_injector import FlaskInjector
from injector import inject
from config import Config

app = Flask(__name__)

@app.route('/config')
@inject
def get_config(config: Config):
```

```
    return jsonify({'environment':
config.ENVIRONMENT})

def configure(binder):
    binder.bind(Config, to=Config())

FlaskInjector(app=app, modules=[configure])

if __name__ == '__main__':
    app.run(debug=True)
```

In this code:

- We define a route `/config` that calls the `get_config()` function to retrieve configuration settings.

- The `get_config()` function takes an instance of `Config` as an argument, which is injected using the `@inject` decorator.

- We define a `configure()` function that binds the `Config` class to an instance of `Config`.

4. Testing with Dependency Injection

One of the key benefits of dependency injection is its ability to facilitate testing by allowing dependencies to be easily replaced with mock objects. Let's look at an example of testing a route handler that depends on a service class:

```python
import pytest
from app import app
from services import UserService

@pytest.fixture
def client():
    with app.test_client() as client:
        yield client

def test_get_users(client, mocker):
    mocker.patch.object(UserService, 'get_all_users', return_value=[{'id': 1, 'username': 'john'}, {'id': 2, 'username': 'jane'}])
    response = client.get('/users')
    assert response.status_code == 200
    assert response.json == [{'id': 1, 'username': 'john'}, {'id': 2, 'username': 'jane'}]
```

In this test:

- We use pytest fixtures to set up a Flask test client.

- We mock the `get_all_users()` method of the `UserService` class using the `mocker` fixture from the pytest-mock package.

- We send a GET request to the `/users` route and verify that the response contains the expected user data.

5. Best Practices for Dependency Injection in Flask

When using dependency injection in your Flask API, consider the following best practices:

- **Use Constructor Injection:** Prefer injecting dependencies via constructor parameters rather than accessing them directly. This promotes explicit dependency declaration and makes it easier to understand component dependencies.

- **Keep Dependencies Explicit:** Clearly define and document the dependencies of each component to avoid ambiguity and confusion.

- **Use Dependency Injection Containers:** Use dependency injection containers like Flask-

Injector or Flask-DI to manage dependencies and facilitate injection throughout your Flask application.

- **Mock Dependencies for Testing:** Use mocking frameworks like pytest-mock to replace real dependencies with mock objects during testing. This allows you to isolate components and test them in isolation.

- **Avoid Circular Dependencies:** Be cautious of circular dependencies between components, as they can lead to complex and error-prone code. Strive to keep dependencies acyclic and well-organized.

Dependency injection is a powerful technique for improving the maintainability, testability, and scalability of your Flask API. By decoupling components and injecting their dependencies, you can create cleaner, more modular code that is easier to understand, maintain, and test. Follow best practices and leverage tools like Flask-Injector to incorporate dependency injection into your Flask projects effectively. With dependency injection, you'll be well-equipped to build robust and maintainable Flask APIs that meet the needs of your users and developers alike.

Configuration Management: Keeping Secrets Secret

In Flask API development, managing configuration settings securely is crucial for maintaining the integrity and security of your application. Flask provides built-in mechanisms for configuration management, allowing you to store sensitive information such as database credentials, API keys, and other secrets securely. In this guide, we'll explore best practices for configuration management in Flask APIs and demonstrate how to keep your secrets safe.

1. Configuration Variables in Flask

Flask uses configuration variables to manage application settings such as debug mode, database URIs, and secret keys. These variables can be set in various ways, including:

- Directly in Python code.

- Using environment variables.

- Loading from configuration files.

Let's start with a basic example of setting configuration variables directly in Python code:

```python
from flask import Flask

app = Flask(__name__)
app.config['SECRET_KEY'] = 'mysecretkey'
app.config['DEBUG'] = True
app.config['DATABASE_URI'] = 'sqlite:///mydatabase.db'
```

In this code:

- We import the `Flask` class from the `flask` module.

- We create an instance of the `Flask` class and assign it to the `app` variable.

- We set configuration variables using the `app.config` dictionary.

2. Using Environment Variables for Configuration

Storing sensitive configuration settings directly in code is not recommended, as it can expose your secrets if your code is shared or version-controlled publicly. Instead, it's best to use environment variables to store sensitive information. Flask provides a convenient way to load configuration from environment variables using the `from_envvar()` method:

```python
from flask import Flask

app = Flask(__name__)
app.config.from_envvar('MYAPP_CONFIG_FILE')
```

In this code:

- We use the `from_envvar()` method to load configuration settings from the `MYAPP_CONFIG_FILE` environment variable.

3. Storing Secrets Securely

When using environment variables for configuration, it's important to ensure that sensitive information such as secret keys and database credentials are stored securely. Avoid hardcoding secrets directly in environment variables or configuration files, as they can be easily exposed. Instead, consider using a secure secrets management solution such as HashiCorp Vault or AWS Secrets Manager to store and retrieve secrets securely.

Here's an example of how you can load secrets from an environment variable using Flask:

```python
import os
from flask import Flask

app = Flask(__name__)
app.config['SECRET_KEY'] = os.getenv('SECRET_KEY')
app.config['DATABASE_URI'] = os.getenv('DATABASE_URI')
```

In this code:

- We use the `os.getenv()` function to retrieve sensitive information from environment variables.

4. Configuration Files

Another common approach to configuration management in Flask is to use configuration files. Flask supports configuration files in various formats such as Python files, JSON files, or YAML files. Here's an example of loading configuration from a Python file:

config.py:

```python
SECRET_KEY = 'mysecretkey'
DEBUG = True
DATABASE_URI = 'sqlite:///mydatabase.db'
```

app.py:

```python
from flask import Flask

app = Flask(__name__)
app.config.from_pyfile('config.py')
```

In this code:

- We create a Python file `config.py` containing configuration settings.

- We use the `from_pyfile()` method to load configuration from the `config.py` file.

5. Best Practices for Configuration Management

To ensure secure and maintainable configuration management in your Flask API, consider the following best practices:

- **Use Environment Variables for Secrets:** Store sensitive information such as secret keys and database credentials in environment variables rather than directly in code or configuration files.

- **Use Different Configuration Sets for Different Environments:** Maintain separate configuration sets for development, testing, and production environments to ensure consistency and security across environments.

- **Encrypt Configuration Files:** If you choose to use configuration files, consider encrypting them to prevent unauthorized access to sensitive information.

- **Rotate Secrets Regularly:** Rotate your secrets (e.g., secret keys, API keys, database credentials) regularly to minimize the risk of exposure in case of a security breach.

- **Limit Access to Configuration:** Restrict access to configuration settings and secrets to authorized personnel only. Implement role-based access control (RBAC) to manage access permissions effectively.

Configuration management is a critical aspect of Flask API development, enabling you to securely manage application settings and sensitive information. By following best practices and leveraging Flask's built-in configuration mechanisms, you can keep your secrets safe and ensure the integrity and security of your Flask applications. Whether you choose to store configuration settings in environment variables, configuration files, or a secure secrets management solution, prioritize security and maintainability to build robust and reliable Flask APIs.

Chapter 3

RESTful Design Principles: Building a Consistent and Predictable API

Creating RESTful endpoints with Flask involves adhering to certain design principles to ensure consistency and predictability in your API. Let's dive into building a Flask API using best practices for RESTful design.

RESTful Endpoints with Flask

Setting Up Flask

First, let's set up a basic Flask application:

```python
from flask import Flask, jsonify, request

app = Flask(__name__)

# Dummy data for demonstration purposes
books = [
    {"id": 1, "title": "Python Programming", "author": "Guido van Rossum"},
    {"id": 2, "title": "Flask Essentials", "author": "Armin Ronacher"}
```

]

```
# Endpoint to get all books
@app.route('/books', methods=['GET'])
def get_books():
    return jsonify(books)

# Endpoint to get a specific book by ID
@app.route('/books/<int:book_id>', methods=['GET'])
def get_book(book_id):
    book = next((book for book in books if book['id'] == book_id), None)
    if book:
        return jsonify(book)
    else:
        return jsonify({"error": "Book not found"}), 404

# Endpoint to create a new book
@app.route('/books', methods=['POST'])
def create_book():
    new_book = request.json
    if 'title' in new_book and 'author' in new_book:
        new_book['id'] = max(book['id'] for book in books) + 1
        books.append(new_book)
        return jsonify(new_book), 201
    else:
```

```
        return jsonify({"error": "Title and author are required"}), 400

# Endpoint to update an existing book
@app.route('/books/<int:book_id>', methods=['PUT'])
def update_book(book_id):
    book = next((book for book in books if book['id'] == book_id), None)
    if book:
        data = request.json
        book.update(data)
        return jsonify(book)
    else:
        return jsonify({"error": "Book not found"}), 404

# Endpoint to delete a book
@app.route('/books/<int:book_id>', methods=['DELETE'])
def delete_book(book_id):
    global books
    books = [book for book in books if book['id'] != book_id]
    return '', 204

if __name__ == '__main__':
    app.run(debug=True)
```

RESTful Design Principles

1. Resource Naming

Resources should be nouns, and the URL should represent the resource hierarchy. For example, `/books` represents a collection of books, while `/books/<book_id>` represents a specific book.

2. HTTP Methods

Use HTTP methods appropriately to perform CRUD (Create, Read, Update, Delete) operations on resources:

- **GET**: Retrieve a resource or a collection of resources.

- **POST**: Create a new resource.

- **PUT**: Update an existing resource.

- **DELETE**: Delete a resource.

3. Use of Status Codes

Return appropriate HTTP status codes to indicate the success or failure of an operation:

- **200 OK:** Successful GET request.

- **201 Created:** Successful POST request.

- **204 No Content:** Successful DELETE request.

- **400 Bad Request:** Invalid request format or missing parameters.

- **404 Not Found:** Resource not found.

- **405 Method Not Allowed**: Request method not supported for the resource.

4. Use of JSON

JSON (JavaScript Object Notation) is a widely accepted format for data exchange in RESTful APIs. Use JSON for request and response payloads to ensure interoperability and ease of parsing.

5. Error Handling

Handle errors gracefully and return informative error messages along with appropriate status codes to help clients understand and troubleshoot issues.

6. Versioning

Consider versioning your API to allow for future changes without breaking existing clients. You can include the version in the URL or as a header.

By following these RESTful design principles and implementing them in your Flask API, you can create a consistent and predictable interface that is easy to understand and use. Remember to test your API thoroughly and document it effectively to guide users in its usage.

HTTP Methods: Verbs that Make Your API Dance (GET, POST, PUT, DELETE)

HTTP methods, also known as verbs, are fundamental to building RESTful APIs with Flask. Each method serves a specific purpose in interacting with resources. Let's explore the four primary HTTP methods: GET, POST, PUT, and DELETE, and how to implement them in a Flask API following best practices.

HTTP Methods in Flask API Development

1. GET Method

The GET method is used to retrieve data from a server. In a Flask API, it's commonly used to fetch resources or collections of resources.

```python
from flask import Flask, jsonify

app = Flask(__name__)

books = [
    {"id": 1, "title": "Python Programming", "author": "Guido van Rossum"},
    {"id": 2, "title": "Flask Essentials", "author": "Armin Ronacher"}
]

@app.route('/books', methods=['GET'])
def get_books():
    return jsonify(books)

if __name__ == '__main__':
    app.run(debug=True)
```

2. POST Method

The POST method is used to create new resources on the server. In Flask, it's typically used to add data to a collection.

```python
from flask import Flask, jsonify, request

app = Flask(__name__)

books = [
    {"id": 1, "title": "Python Programming", "author": "Guido van Rossum"},
    {"id": 2, "title": "Flask Essentials", "author": "Armin Ronacher"}
]

@app.route('/books', methods=['POST'])
def create_book():
    new_book = request.json
    if 'title' in new_book and 'author' in new_book:
        new_book['id'] = max(book['id'] for book in books) + 1
        books.append(new_book)
        return jsonify(new_book), 201
    else:
        return jsonify({"error": "Title and author are required"}), 400
```

```
if __name__ == '__main__':
    app.run(debug=True)
```

3. PUT Method

The PUT method is used to update existing resources on the server. In Flask, it's commonly used to modify specific resources identified by their IDs.

```python
from flask import Flask, jsonify, request

app = Flask(__name__)

books = [
    {"id": 1, "title": "Python Programming", "author": "Guido van Rossum"},
    {"id": 2, "title": "Flask Essentials", "author": "Armin Ronacher"}
]

@app.route('/books/<int:book_id>', methods=['PUT'])
def update_book(book_id):
    book = next((book for book in books if book['id'] == book_id), None)
    if book:
        data = request.json
```

```
        book.update(data)
        return jsonify(book)
    else:
        return jsonify({"error": "Book not found"}), 404

if __name__ == '__main__':
    app.run(debug=True)
```

4. DELETE Method

The DELETE method is used to remove resources from the server. In Flask, it's commonly used to delete specific resources identified by their IDs.

```python
from flask import Flask, jsonify

app = Flask(__name__)

books = [
    {"id": 1, "title": "Python Programming", "author": "Guido van Rossum"},
    {"id": 2, "title": "Flask Essentials", "author": "Armin Ronacher"}
]
```

```
@app.route('/books/<int:book_id>',
methods=['DELETE'])
def delete_book(book_id):
    global books
    books = [book for book in books if book['id'] != book_id]
    return '', 204

if __name__ == '__main__':
    app.run(debug=True)
```

Best Practices for Flask API Development

1. Use Appropriate HTTP Status Codes: Return meaningful status codes like 200 for successful requests, 201 for created resources, 404 for not found, and 400 for bad requests.

2. Input Validation: Validate input data to ensure it meets the expected format and requirements.

3. Error Handling: Implement robust error handling to provide descriptive error messages in case of failures.

4. Security: Implement authentication and authorization mechanisms to protect your API from unauthorized access.

5. Documentation: Document your API endpoints, request payloads, and response formats using tools like Swagger or OpenAPI.

6. Testing: Write comprehensive unit tests to ensure the reliability and stability of your API.

7. Versioning: Consider versioning your API to manage changes and backward compatibility.

By following these best practices and implementing HTTP methods effectively in your Flask API, you can create a robust and reliable interface for interacting with your resources. Remember to continuously refine and improve your API based on feedback and evolving requirements.

Resource-Oriented Design: Structuring Endpoints Around Your Data

Resource-oriented design (ROD) is a design approach in which APIs are structured around resources, representing entities or collections of data. This methodology emphasizes organizing endpoints and data models in a way that aligns with the underlying data structure. Let's explore how to implement resource-oriented design in a Flask API using best practices.

Understanding Resource-Oriented Design

In resource-oriented design, each resource is represented by a unique URI (Uniform Resource Identifier), and endpoints are structured around these resources. This approach promotes a clear and intuitive API structure, making it easier for clients to understand and navigate the API.

Structuring Endpoints with Flask

Example: Book Management API

Let's consider a simple example of a book management API. We'll structure our endpoints around the `Book` resource.

```python
from flask import Flask, jsonify, request

app = Flask(__name__)

books = [
    {"id": 1, "title": "Python Programming", "author": "Guido van Rossum"},
    {"id": 2, "title": "Flask Essentials", "author": "Armin Ronacher"}
```

]

```python
# Endpoint to get all books
@app.route('/books', methods=['GET'])
def get_books():
    return jsonify(books)

# Endpoint to get a specific book by ID
@app.route('/books/<int:book_id>', methods=['GET'])
def get_book(book_id):
    book = next((book for book in books if book['id'] == book_id), None)
    if book:
        return jsonify(book)
    else:
        return jsonify({"error": "Book not found"}), 404

# Endpoint to create a new book
@app.route('/books', methods=['POST'])
def create_book():
    new_book = request.json
    if 'title' in new_book and 'author' in new_book:
        new_book['id'] = max(book['id'] for book in books) + 1
        books.append(new_book)
        return jsonify(new_book), 201
    else:
```

```
        return jsonify({"error": "Title and author are required"}), 400

# Endpoint to update an existing book
@app.route('/books/<int:book_id>', methods=['PUT'])
def update_book(book_id):
    book = next((book for book in books if book['id'] == book_id), None)
    if book:
        data = request.json
        book.update(data)
        return jsonify(book)
    else:
        return jsonify({"error": "Book not found"}), 404

# Endpoint to delete a book
@app.route('/books/<int:book_id>', methods=['DELETE'])
def delete_book(book_id):
    global books
    books = [book for book in books if book['id'] != book_id]
    return '', 204

if __name__ == '__main__':
    app.run(debug=True)
```

Best Practices for Resource-Oriented Design in Flask

1. Consistent Naming: Use consistent naming conventions for endpoints and resource identifiers to enhance clarity and maintainability.

2. Use of HTTP Methods: Utilize HTTP methods (GET, POST, PUT, DELETE) appropriately to perform CRUD operations on resources.

3. Resource Identification: Use resource identifiers (IDs) to uniquely identify resources and enable retrieval and manipulation.

4. Input Validation: Validate input data to ensure it meets the expected format and requirements before processing.

5. Error Handling: Implement robust error handling to provide descriptive error messages in case of failures or invalid requests.

6. Security: Implement authentication and authorization mechanisms to protect resources from unauthorized access.

7. Documentation: Document your API endpoints, request payloads, and response formats to guide users in using the API effectively.

Resource-oriented design is a powerful approach for structuring APIs around the underlying data model. By organizing endpoints around resources and following best practices in Flask API development, you can create a clear, intuitive, and maintainable API that effectively exposes your data to clients. Continuously refine and improve your API based on feedback and evolving requirements to ensure its effectiveness and usability.

Versioning Your API: Ensuring Smooth Transitions and Backward Compatibility

Versioning your API is crucial for ensuring smooth transitions and backward compatibility as your API evolves over time. By versioning your API, you allow clients to continue using older versions while adopting new features or changes gradually. Let's explore how to implement versioning in a Flask API using best practices.

Understanding API Versioning

API versioning involves providing a unique identifier for each version of your API. This identifier is typically included in the URL or as a request header. Versioning allows developers to introduce changes, improvements, or new features without breaking existing client implementations.

Implementing Versioning in Flask

Example: Versioned Book Management API

Let's extend our previous example of the book management API to include versioning.

```python
from flask import Flask, jsonify, request

app = Flask(__name__)

# Dummy data for demonstration purposes
books = [
    {"id": 1, "title": "Python Programming", "author": "Guido van Rossum"},
    {"id": 2, "title": "Flask Essentials", "author": "Armin Ronacher"}
]

# Version 1 of the API

@app.route('/v1/books', methods=['GET'])
```

```python
def get_books_v1():
    return jsonify(books)

@app.route('/v1/books/<int:book_id>', methods=['GET'])
def get_book_v1(book_id):
    book = next((book for book in books if book['id'] == book_id), None)
    if book:
        return jsonify(book)
    else:
        return jsonify({"error": "Book not found"}), 404

# Version 2 of the API with additional fields

@app.route('/v2/books', methods=['GET'])
def get_books_v2():
    # Return books with additional fields or modified structure
    pass

@app.route('/v2/books/<int:book_id>', methods=['GET'])
def get_book_v2(book_id):
    # Return book with additional fields or modified structure
    pass
```

```python
# Endpoint to create a new book (versioned)
@app.route('/v1/books', methods=['POST'])
def create_book_v1():
    new_book = request.json
    if 'title' in new_book and 'author' in new_book:
        new_book['id'] = max(book['id'] for book in books) + 1
        books.append(new_book)
        return jsonify(new_book), 201
    else:
        return jsonify({"error": "Title and author are required"}), 400

# Version 2 of the create book endpoint with additional fields
@app.route('/v2/books', methods=['POST'])
def create_book_v2():
    # Handle creating books with additional fields or modified structure
    pass

if __name__ == '__main__':
    app.run(debug=True)
```

Best Practices for API Versioning in Flask

1. Clear Versioning Scheme: Use a clear and consistent versioning scheme, such as "/v1/", "/v2/", etc., in your URL structure.

2. Support for Multiple Versions: Provide support for multiple versions of your API concurrently to allow clients to migrate at their own pace.

3. Granular Versioning: Consider granular versioning to allow for incremental changes and updates within each version.

4. Deprecation Policies: Clearly communicate deprecation policies for older versions of the API to give clients sufficient time to migrate.

5. Semantic Versioning: Follow semantic versioning principles to indicate the nature of changes (major, minor, patch) in each version.

6. Documentation: Document each version of your API thoroughly, including changes, endpoints, request/response formats, and migration guides.

7. Testing: Thoroughly test each version of your API to ensure backward compatibility and prevent regressions.

Versioning your API is essential for maintaining backward compatibility and facilitating smooth transitions as your API evolves. By implementing versioning in your Flask API using best practices, you can provide a stable and reliable interface for clients while introducing changes and improvements iteratively. Continuously monitor usage patterns and gather feedback to inform future versioning decisions and ensure the long-term success of your API.

Chapter 4

Working with Data: From Simple Variables to Databases with SQLAlchemy

Working with data is a fundamental aspect of building Flask APIs, from handling simple variables to utilizing databases for storage. SQLAlchemy is a powerful toolkit and ORM (Object-Relational Mapping) for working with databases in Flask applications. Let's explore how to work with data using SQLAlchemy in Flask API development, following best practices.

Handling Simple Variables

In Flask APIs, handling simple variables involves processing data received in requests and returning data as responses. Let's start with a basic example of a Flask API that handles simple variables:

```python
from flask import Flask, jsonify, request

app = Flask(__name__)

# Dummy data for demonstration purposes
books = []
```

```
# Endpoint to add a new book
@app.route('/books', methods=['POST'])
def add_book():
    data = request.json
    title = data.get('title')
    author = data.get('author')
    if title and author:
        book = {'title': title, 'author': author}
        books.append(book)
        return jsonify({"message": "Book added successfully"}), 201
    else:
        return jsonify({"error": "Title and author are required"}), 400

# Endpoint to get all books
@app.route('/books', methods=['GET'])
def get_books():
    return jsonify(books)

if __name__ == '__main__':
    app.run(debug=True)
```
```

## **Working with Databases Using SQLAlchemy**

As your application grows, you may need to store data in a database for persistence and scalability. SQLAlchemy
```

provides a convenient way to interact with databases in Flask applications. Let's enhance our previous example to use SQLAlchemy with an SQLite database.

```python
from flask import Flask, jsonify, request
from flask_sqlalchemy import SQLAlchemy

app = Flask(__name__)
app.config['SQLALCHEMY_DATABASE_URI'] = 'sqlite:///books.db'
db = SQLAlchemy(app)

# Book model
class Book(db.Model):
    id = db.Column(db.Integer, primary_key=True)
    title = db.Column(db.String(100), nullable=False)
    author = db.Column(db.String(100), nullable=False)

# Endpoint to add a new book
@app.route('/books', methods=['POST'])
def add_book():
    data = request.json
    title = data.get('title')
    author = data.get('author')
    if title and author:
        new_book = Book(title=title, author=author)
        db.session.add(new_book)
```

```
        db.session.commit()
        return jsonify({"message": "Book added successfully"}), 201
    else:
        return jsonify({"error": "Title and author are required"}), 400

# Endpoint to get all books
@app.route('/books', methods=['GET'])
def get_books():
    books = Book.query.all()
    book_list = [{'id': book.id, 'title': book.title, 'author': book.author} for book in books]
    return jsonify(book_list)

if __name__ == '__main__':
    app.run(debug=True)
```

Best Practices for Working with Data in Flask

1. Use Models: Define models to represent your data structures, making it easier to interact with databases and maintain data integrity.

2. Handle Errors: Implement error handling to gracefully handle exceptions and provide informative error messages to clients.

3. Validation: Validate input data to ensure it meets the expected format and constraints before processing.

4. Security: Protect your application against common security vulnerabilities such as SQL injection by using parameterized queries and ORM features provided by SQLAlchemy.

5. Transaction Management: Use transactions to ensure data consistency and atomicity when making changes to the database.

6. Testing: Write comprehensive unit tests to validate data operations and ensure the reliability of your application.

7. Documentation: Document your data models, endpoints, and data manipulation operations to guide developers in using your API effectively.

Working with data in Flask APIs involves handling simple variables and leveraging databases for persistent storage. SQLAlchemy provides a powerful toolkit for interacting with databases in Flask applications, allowing you to define models, execute queries, and manage transactions effectively. By following best practices and guidelines for working with data in Flask, you can build robust and scalable APIs that meet the needs of your users and applications.

Data Validation: Ensuring Your API Receives Clean Data

Data validation is essential for ensuring the integrity and security of your Flask API. By validating incoming data, you can ensure that your API receives clean and formatted data, reducing the risk of errors and security vulnerabilities. Let's explore how to implement data validation in Flask API development using best practices.

Importance of Data Validation

Data validation is crucial for several reasons:

1. Data Integrity: Ensures that data conforms to expected formats and constraints, preventing corrupt or invalid data from entering the system.

2. Security: Helps mitigate security risks such as injection attacks by sanitizing and validating input data.

3. User Experience: Improves the user experience by providing immediate feedback on data entry errors, reducing frustration and improving usability.

4. Compliance: Ensures compliance with data validation requirements mandated by regulations or industry standards.

Implementing Data Validation in Flask

Using Flask-WTF for Form Validation

Flask-WTF is an extension for Flask that provides integration with WTForms, a flexible form validation and rendering library for Python web development. Let's see how to use Flask-WTF for data validation in a Flask API:

```python
from flask import Flask, jsonify, request
from flask_wtf import FlaskForm
from wtforms import StringField, validators

app = Flask(__name__)
app.config['SECRET_KEY'] = 'secret_key'

# Define a form for data validation
class BookForm(FlaskForm):
    title = StringField('Title', validators=[validators.InputRequired()])
```

```python
    author = StringField('Author', validators=[validators.InputRequired()])

# Endpoint to add a new book
@app.route('/books', methods=['POST'])
def add_book():
    form = BookForm(request.form)
    if form.validate():
        title = form.title.data
        author = form.author.data
        # Process the data
        return jsonify({"message": "Book added successfully"}), 201
    else:
        errors = form.errors
        return jsonify({"error": errors}), 400

if __name__ == '__main__':
    app.run(debug=True)
```

Using Manual Validation

If you prefer not to use Flask-WTF or WTForms, you can perform manual data validation using Flask's request object:

```python
```

```python
from flask import Flask, jsonify, request

app = Flask(__name__)

# Endpoint to add a new book
@app.route('/books', methods=['POST'])
def add_book():
    data = request.json
    title = data.get('title')
    author = data.get('author')
    if title and author:
        # Process the data
        return jsonify({"message": "Book added successfully"}), 201
    else:
        return jsonify({"error": "Title and author are required"}), 400

if __name__ == '__main__':
    app.run(debug=True)
```

Best Practices for Data Validation in Flask

1. Use Input Validation Libraries: Leverage libraries like Flask-WTF or WTForms for comprehensive input validation and error handling.

2. Sanitize Input: Sanitize input data to remove potentially harmful characters or content before processing.

3. Define Validation Rules: Clearly define validation rules and constraints for each data field to ensure consistency and data integrity.

4. Handle Errors Gracefully: Provide clear and informative error messages to users when validation fails, helping them understand and correct input errors.

5. Use HTTPS: Transmit data securely over HTTPS to prevent eavesdropping and tampering during data transmission.

6. Implement Server-Side Validation: Always perform data validation on the server-side to prevent bypassing client-side validation and ensure security.

7. Continuous Testing: Continuously test your API endpoints with various input scenarios to identify and fix validation issues.

Data validation is a critical aspect of Flask API development, ensuring that your API receives clean and formatted data. By implementing data validation using Flask-WTF, WTForms, or manual validation techniques, you can enhance the integrity, security, and usability of your API. Follow best practices for data validation to mitigate risks, improve user experience, and comply with regulatory requirements effectively.

Serialization: Transforming Data for Seamless Consumption by Clients

Serialization is the process of converting complex data structures into a format that can be easily transmitted and interpreted by clients. In Flask API development, serialization is crucial for transforming data into formats such as JSON or XML for seamless consumption by clients. Let's explore how to implement serialization in Flask APIs using best practices, with a focus on Webster, a lightweight serialization library for Flask.

Understanding Serialization

Serialization plays a vital role in API development for several reasons:

1. Interoperability: By serializing data into common formats like JSON or XML, APIs can communicate with a wide range of clients, regardless of their programming language or platform.

2. Efficiency: Serialized data is compact and lightweight, making it efficient to transmit over the network, reducing bandwidth usage and improving performance.

3. Data Transformation: Serialization allows developers to transform complex data structures into simpler formats that are easier to work with on the client side.

Implementing Serialization in Flask with Webster

Webster is a Flask extension that provides serialization capabilities for Flask APIs. It simplifies the process of serializing and deserializing data, allowing developers to focus on building robust APIs. Let's see how to use Webster for serialization in a Flask API:

Installation

First, install Webster using pip:

```
pip install flask-webster
```

Usage

```python
from flask import Flask
from flask_webster import Webster

app = Flask(__name__)
webster = Webster(app)

# Define a data model
class Book:
    def __init__(self, title, author):
        self.title = title
        self.author = author

# Endpoint to get a book
@app.route('/books/<int:book_id>')
def get_book(book_id):
    # Retrieve book data from database or other source
    book_data = {'title': 'Python Programming', 'author': 'Guido van Rossum'}
    book = Book(**book_data)
    return webster.jsonify(book)

if __name__ == '__main__':
    app.run(debug=True)
```

In this example, we define a `Book` class representing a data model. The `get_book` endpoint retrieves book data and serializes it into JSON format using Webster's `jsonify` method.

Best Practices for Serialization in Flask

1. Consistent Data Structures: Define consistent data structures and models to ensure uniform serialization across endpoints.

2. Use of Libraries: Leverage serialization libraries like Webster or Flask's built-in `jsonify` to simplify serialization tasks and ensure consistency.

3. Custom Serialization: Implement custom serialization methods for complex data structures or cases where default serialization is insufficient.

4. Error Handling*: Handle errors gracefully during serialization and provide informative error messages to clients in case of failures.

5. Performance Optimization: Optimize serialization performance by minimizing the size of serialized data and reducing unnecessary overhead.

6. Data Integrity: Ensure data integrity during serialization by validating input data and sanitizing inputs to prevent injection attacks or data corruption.

7. Versioning: Consider versioning your serialization formats to support backward compatibility and allow for future changes without breaking existing clients.

Serialization is a critical aspect of Flask API development, enabling seamless communication between clients and servers. By implementing serialization using libraries like Webster and following best practices, you can ensure efficient data transmission, interoperability, and data integrity in your Flask APIs. Serialization simplifies the process of transforming complex data structures into formats that can be easily consumed and interpreted by clients, improving the overall user experience and performance of your API.

Common Data Formats: JSON, XML, and Beyond

Common data formats like JSON (JavaScript Object Notation) and XML (eXtensible Markup Language) play a crucial role in web development, especially in Flask API development. These formats enable data interchange between clients and servers in a standardized and efficient manner. Let's explore JSON, XML, and other common data formats, along with how to handle them in Flask APIs using best practices.

Introduction to Data Formats

Data formats define the structure and representation of data exchanged between systems. They facilitate interoperability, ease of parsing, and efficient transmission of data over the network. Here are some common data formats used in web development:

1. JSON (JavaScript Object Notation): A lightweight data interchange format that is easy for humans to read and write and easy for machines to parse and generate. It is widely used in web APIs due to its simplicity and flexibility.

2. XML (eXtensible Markup Language): A markup language that defines a set of rules for encoding documents in a format that is both human-readable and machine-readable. XML is more verbose than JSON but offers strong support for structured data and metadata.

3. CSV (Comma-Separated Values): A simple tabular data format with fields separated by commas. CSV is commonly used for exporting and importing data between different applications and systems.

4. YAML (YAML Ain't Markup Language): A human-readable data serialization format that is often used for configuration files and data exchange between systems.

Handling Common Data Formats in Flask

Flask provides built-in support for handling common data formats such as JSON and XML. Let's explore how to handle these formats in a Flask API:

JSON Format

JSON is the most common data format used in Flask APIs due to its simplicity and widespread support. Flask provides the `jsonify` function for serializing Python data structures to JSON format.

```python
from flask import Flask, jsonify

app = Flask(__name__)

# Endpoint to return JSON data
@app.route('/json', methods=['GET'])
def get_json_data():
    data = {'name': 'John', 'age': 30, 'city': 'New York'}
    return jsonify(data)

if __name__ == '__main__':
```

```
    app.run(debug=True)
```

XML Format

While JSON is more commonly used in Flask APIs, Flask also supports handling XML data using the `xmlify` function provided by the `Flask-XML` extension.

```python
from flask import Flask
from flask_xml import FlaskXML

app = Flask(__name__)
xml = FlaskXML(app)

# Endpoint to return XML data
@app.route('/xml', methods=['GET'])
def get_xml_data():
    xml_data = '<person><name>John</name><age>30</age><city>New York</city></person>'
    return xml.xmlify(xml_data)

if __name__ == '__main__':
    app.run(debug=True)
```

Other Data Formats

For handling CSV, YAML, or other data formats in Flask, you can use third-party libraries or implement custom serialization and deserialization methods as needed.

Best Practices for Handling Data Formats in Flask

1. Consistent Data Formats: Choose a consistent data format (e.g., JSON) for your API responses to simplify client-side parsing and ensure interoperability.

2. Error Handling: Implement robust error handling mechanisms to handle parsing errors and provide informative error messages to clients.

3. Content Negotiation: Support content negotiation to allow clients to specify their preferred data format using HTTP headers (e.g., `Accept` header).

4. Security Considerations: Validate and sanitize input data to prevent injection attacks and ensure data integrity when handling different data formats.

5. Performance Optimization: Optimize data serialization and deserialization processes for performance by minimizing unnecessary overhead and processing.

6. Documentation: Document the supported data formats, their structure, and any specific requirements for data interchange in your API documentation.

7. Testing: Test your API endpoints with different data formats and edge cases to ensure compatibility and reliability across different clients and scenarios.

Understanding and effectively handling common data formats like JSON, XML, CSV, and YAML is essential for Flask API development. By following best practices and leveraging Flask's built-in support or third-party extensions, you can ensure seamless data interchange between your API and clients. Consistent data formats, robust error handling, and performance optimization are key considerations for designing and implementing APIs that meet the needs of modern web applications.

Chapter 5

Understanding Authentication Mechanisms: Basic, Token-Based, and More

Understanding authentication mechanisms is crucial for securing Flask APIs and controlling access to resources. There are several authentication methods available, including basic authentication, token-based authentication, OAuth, and more. Let's explore these authentication mechanisms, along with code examples and best practices for implementing them in Flask API development.

1. Basic Authentication

Basic authentication is a simple authentication mechanism where the client sends the username and password with each request. The server validates the credentials and grants access if they are correct.

```python
from flask import Flask, jsonify, request
from flask_httpauth import HTTPBasicAuth

app = Flask(__name__)
auth = HTTPBasicAuth()
```

```python
# Dummy user data (replace with actual user data)
users = {
    'john': 'secret',
    'jane': 'password'
}

@auth.verify_password
def verify_password(username, password):
    if username in users and users[username] == password:
        return username

@app.route('/private')
@auth.login_required
def private_endpoint():
    return jsonify({"message": "Access granted for {}".format(auth.current_user())})

if __name__ == '__main__':
    app.run(debug=True)
```

In this example, we use the `HTTPBasicAuth` extension to implement basic authentication. The `verify_password` callback verifies the username and password against a dictionary of user credentials.

2. Token-Based Authentication

Token-based authentication involves issuing a token to the client upon successful login. The client sends this token with each request, and the server validates it to grant access.

```python
from flask import Flask, jsonify, request
from flask_jwt_extended import JWTManager, create_access_token, jwt_required, get_jwt_identity

app = Flask(__name__)
app.config['JWT_SECRET_KEY'] = 'secret_key'
jwt = JWTManager(app)

# Dummy user data (replace with actual user data)
users = {
    'john': 'password',
    'jane': 'password123'
}

@app.route('/login', methods=['POST'])
def login():
    data = request.json
    username = data.get('username')
    password = data.get('password')
    if username in users and users[username] == password:
```

```
        access_token =
create_access_token(identity=username)
        return jsonify(access_token=access_token)
    else:
        return jsonify({"error": "Invalid username or
password"}), 401

@app.route('/private')
@jwt_required()
def private_endpoint():
    current_user = get_jwt_identity()
    return jsonify({"message": "Access granted for
{}".format(current_user)})

if __name__ == '__main__':
    app.run(debug=True)
```

Here, we use the `Flask-JWT-Extended` extension to implement token-based authentication. The `/login` endpoint issues a JWT token upon successful login, which the client sends with subsequent requests to access protected resources.

3. OAuth

OAuth is an authentication protocol that allows users to grant third-party applications limited access to their resources without sharing their credentials. OAuth involves three parties: the client (application), the resource owner (user), and the authorization server.

```python
# Flask-OAuthlib example code
from flask import Flask, jsonify, redirect, url_for
from flask_oauthlib.client import OAuth

app = Flask(__name__)
app.config['SECRET_KEY'] = 'secret_key'
app.config['OAUTH1_PROVIDER_ENFORCE_SSL'] = False
oauth = OAuth(app)

twitter = oauth.remote_app(
    'twitter',
    consumer_key='your-consumer-key',
    consumer_secret='your-consumer-secret',
    request_token_params={'scope': 'read'},
    base_url='https://api.twitter.com/1.1/',

request_token_url='https://api.twitter.com/oauth/request_token',

access_token_url='https://api.twitter.com/oauth/access_token',
```

```
    authorize_url='https://api.twitter.com/oauth/authenticate'
)

@app.route('/login')
def login():
    return twitter.authorize(callback=url_for('oauth_authorized',
        next=request.args.get('next') or request.referrer or None))

@app.route('/oauth-authorized')
@twitter.authorized_handler
def oauth_authorized(resp):
    if resp is None:
        return 'Access denied: reason={}, error={}'.format(
            request.args['error_reason'],
            request.args['error_description']
        )
    return jsonify(resp)

if __name__ == '__main__':
    app.run(debug=True)
```

In this example, we use the `Flask-OAuthlib` extension to implement OAuth authentication with Twitter as the provider. The `/login` endpoint initiates the OAuth flow, and the `/oauth-authorized` endpoint handles the callback from Twitter.

Best Practices for Authentication in Flask

1. Use HTTPS: Always use HTTPS to encrypt communication between the client and server, preventing eavesdropping and data tampering.

2. Secure Password Storage: Store passwords securely using hashing algorithms like bcrypt to protect user credentials.

3. Rate Limiting: Implement rate limiting to prevent brute-force attacks and protect against denial-of-service (DoS) attacks.

4. Session Management: Use secure session management techniques to maintain user sessions and prevent session hijacking.

5. Custom Error Messages: Provide informative error messages to clients to help them understand and troubleshoot authentication failures.

6. Multi-Factor Authentication (MFA): Consider implementing multi-factor authentication for added security, especially for sensitive operations.

7. Continuous Monitoring: Monitor authentication logs and metrics regularly to detect and respond to suspicious activities or security incidents.

Authentication is a critical aspect of Flask API development, ensuring that only authorized users can access protected resources. By understanding and implementing various authentication mechanisms such as basic authentication, token-based authentication, and OAuth, you can secure your Flask APIs effectively. Follow best practices for authentication, including HTTPS usage, secure password storage, rate limiting, and session management, to enhance the security and reliability of your APIs.

Implementing Authentication with Flask Extensions

Implementing authentication in Flask APIs can be streamlined and simplified using various Flask extensions specifically designed for this purpose. These extensions provide pre-built solutions for common authentication mechanisms such as JWT (JSON Web Tokens), OAuth, and more. Let's explore how to implement authentication using Flask extensions, along with code examples and best practices for Flask API development.

Introduction to Flask Extensions for Authentication

Flask extensions offer convenient and efficient ways to implement authentication in Flask APIs. These extensions handle common authentication tasks such as user management, token generation, and session handling, allowing developers to focus on building their APIs rather than reinventing authentication mechanisms from scratch. Here are some popular Flask extensions for authentication:

1. Flask-JWT-Extended: Provides JWT-based authentication and token management for Flask APIs.

2. Flask-OAuthlib: Implements OAuth authentication protocol, allowing users to authorize third-party applications to access their resources.

3. Flask-Login: Offers user session management and authentication for Flask applications.

4. Flask-Security: A comprehensive security extension for Flask that includes features like user authentication, role-based access control, password hashing, and more.

Implementing Authentication with Flask-JWT-Extended

Flask-JWT-Extended is a popular extension for implementing token-based authentication in Flask APIs. It provides functionality for issuing JWT tokens upon user authentication and validating these tokens for accessing protected resources.

Installation

First, install Flask-JWT-Extended using pip:

```
pip install flask-jwt-extended
```

Example Code

```python
from flask import Flask, jsonify, request
from flask_jwt_extended import JWTManager, jwt_required, create_access_token, get_jwt_identity

app = Flask(__name__)
app.config['JWT_SECRET_KEY'] = 'secret_key'
jwt = JWTManager(app)

# Dummy user data (replace with actual user data)
users = {
```

```
    'john': 'password',
    'jane': 'password123'
}

@app.route('/login', methods=['POST'])
def login():
    data = request.json
    username = data.get('username')
    password = data.get('password')
    if username in users and users[username] == password:
        access_token = create_access_token(identity=username)
        return jsonify(access_token=access_token)
    else:
        return jsonify({"error": "Invalid username or password"}), 401

@app.route('/private')
@jwt_required()
def private_endpoint():
    current_user = get_jwt_identity()
    return jsonify({"message": "Access granted for {}".format(current_user)})

if __name__ == '__main__':
    app.run(debug=True)
```

In this example, we use Flask-JWT-Extended to implement token-based authentication. The `/login` endpoint authenticates users and issues JWT tokens upon successful login. The `/private` endpoint requires a valid JWT token for access.

Best Practices for Implementing Authentication with Flask Extensions

1. Secure Token Storage: Store JWT tokens securely on the client side to prevent unauthorized access or tampering.

2. Token Expiration: Set a reasonable expiration time for JWT tokens to limit their validity and reduce the risk of misuse.

3. User Authentication: Implement strong password policies and user authentication mechanisms to prevent unauthorized access.

4. Rate Limiting: Apply rate limiting to authentication endpoints to prevent brute-force attacks and protect against DoS attacks.

5. Error Handling: Provide informative error messages to users in case of authentication failures or invalid tokens.

6. HTTPS Usage: Always use HTTPS to encrypt communication between the client and server, especially when transmitting sensitive authentication data.

7. Session Management: Implement secure session management techniques to maintain user sessions and prevent session hijacking.

Flask extensions offer convenient and efficient ways to implement authentication in Flask APIs, allowing developers to focus on building their APIs rather than dealing with authentication complexities. By leveraging extensions like Flask-JWT-Extended, Flask-OAuthlib, or Flask-Security, you can implement authentication mechanisms such as token-based authentication or OAuth with ease. Follow best practices for authentication, including token security, user authentication, rate limiting, and error handling, to ensure the security and reliability of your Flask APIs.

Session Management: Keeping Users Logged In

Session management is crucial for maintaining user authentication and state in Flask APIs, especially for web applications that require users to log in and access protected resources. Flask provides various mechanisms for managing sessions, including Flask-Login and Flask-Session extensions. Let's explore how to implement session management in Flask APIs, along with code examples and best practices for Flask API development.

Introduction to Session Management in Flask

Session management involves maintaining user sessions and state information between client requests and server responses. This is typically achieved by using session cookies or tokens to identify authenticated users and store session data on the server side.

Using Flask-Login for Session Management

Flask-Login is a popular extension for managing user sessions and authentication in Flask applications. It provides functionality for user login, logout, session management, and access control.

Installation

First, install Flask-Login using pip:

```
pip install flask-login
```

Example Code

```python
from flask import Flask, jsonify, request, session, redirect, url_for
from flask_login import LoginManager, UserMixin, login_user, logout_user, login_required

app = Flask(__name__)
app.secret_key = 'secret_key'
login_manager = LoginManager(app)

# Dummy user data (replace with actual user data)
users = {
    'john': {'password': 'password'},
    'jane': {'password': 'password123'}
}

# User model
class User(UserMixin):
    pass
```

```python
@login_manager.user_loader
def load_user(username):
    if username in users:
        user = User()
        user.id = username
        return user

@app.route('/login', methods=['POST'])
def login():
    data = request.json
    username = data.get('username')
    password = data.get('password')
    if username in users and users[username]['password'] == password:
        user = User()
        user.id = username
        login_user(user)
        return jsonify({"message": "Login successful"})
    else:
        return jsonify({"error": "Invalid username or password"}), 401

@app.route('/logout')
@login_required
def logout():
    logout_user()
    return jsonify({"message": "Logout successful"})
```

```
@app.route('/private')
@login_required
def private_endpoint():
    return jsonify({"message": "Access granted for {}".format(session['user_id'])})

if __name__ == '__main__':
    app.run(debug=True)
```

In this example, we use Flask-Login to manage user sessions and authentication. The `/login` endpoint authenticates users and logs them in using the `login_user` function. The `/logout` endpoint logs users out using the `logout_user` function. The `/private` endpoint requires users to be logged in using the `login_required` decorator.

Best Practices for Session Management in Flask

1. Secure Session Cookies: Set the `SESSION_COOKIE_SECURE` configuration option to `True` to ensure that session cookies are only sent over HTTPS connections.

2. Session Expiration: Set a reasonable session expiration time to limit the lifetime of user sessions and reduce the risk of session hijacking.

3. Session Storage: Store session data securely on the server side or use signed cookies to prevent tampering by clients.

4. Logout Mechanism: Implement a proper logout mechanism to invalidate user sessions and remove session data from the server side.

5. User Authentication: Use strong password policies and implement robust user authentication mechanisms to prevent unauthorized access.

6. Error Handling: Provide informative error messages to users in case of authentication failures or session expiration.

7. Session Persistence: Consider using session persistence mechanisms like Redis or database-backed sessions for scalability and reliability.

Session management is an essential aspect of Flask API development, ensuring that users can authenticate and access protected resources securely. By leveraging Flask extensions like Flask-Login, you can implement session management functionality with ease, including user login, logout, and access control. Follow best practices for session management, including secure session cookies, session expiration, and proper logout mechanisms, to ensure the security and reliability of your Flask APIs.

Chapter 6

Role-Based Access Control (RBAC): Granular Control Over User Permissions

Role-Based Access Control (RBAC) is a powerful method for managing user permissions and access control in Flask APIs. RBAC allows administrators to assign roles to users, and each role has specific permissions associated with it. Users are then granted access to resources based on their assigned roles. Let's explore how to implement RBAC in Flask APIs, along with code examples and best practices for Flask API development.

Introduction to Role-Based Access Control (RBAC)

RBAC is a widely adopted access control model that provides a flexible and scalable way to manage user permissions in web applications. In RBAC, permissions are grouped into roles, and users are assigned one or more roles based on their responsibilities or privileges. This approach simplifies access control management and ensures that users only have access to the resources and actions that are necessary for their roles.

Implementing RBAC in Flask APIs

To implement RBAC in Flask APIs, we need to define roles, permissions, and mechanisms for assigning roles to users and checking permissions for accessing resources.

Example Code

```python
from flask import Flask, jsonify, request
from functools import wraps

app = Flask(__name__)

# Dummy user data (replace with actual user data)
users = {
    'john': {'password': 'password', 'roles': ['admin']},
    'jane': {'password': 'password123', 'roles': ['user']}
}

# Dummy role permissions (replace with actual permissions)
role_permissions = {
    'admin': ['read', 'write', 'delete'],
    'user': ['read']
}

# Custom decorator to check permissions
def has_permission(permission):
```

```
    def decorator(func):
        @wraps(func)
        def wrapper(*args, **kwargs):
            user_roles = users.get(request.authorization.username).get('roles')
            if permission in role_permissions.get(user_roles[0]):
                return func(*args, **kwargs)
            else:
                return jsonify({"error": "Insufficient permissions"}), 403
        return wrapper
    return decorator

# Protected endpoint with permission check
@app.route('/protected')
@has_permission('read')
def protected_endpoint():
    return jsonify({"message": "Access granted"})

if __name__ == '__main__':
    app.run(debug=True)
```

In this example, we define a custom decorator `has_permission` that checks if the user has the required permission based on their assigned role. The `protected_endpoint` is a sample protected endpoint where access is granted only to users with the "read" permission.

Best Practices for Implementing RBAC in Flask

1. Granular Permissions: Define granular permissions to provide fine-grained control over user access to resources and actions.

2. Role Hierarchy: Establish a role hierarchy if necessary to manage inheritance of permissions and roles.

3. Centralized Role Management: Centralize role management and permissions to simplify administration and ensure consistency.

4. Secure Role Assignment: Ensure secure assignment of roles to users and validate user permissions before granting access to resources.

5. Error Handling: Implement proper error handling mechanisms to handle permission errors and provide informative error messages to users.

6. Regular Auditing: Regularly audit user roles and permissions to ensure that access control policies are up-to-date and effective.

7. Testing: Test RBAC functionality thoroughly to verify that users are granted appropriate access based on their roles and permissions.

Role-Based Access Control (RBAC) is an effective method for managing user permissions and access control in Flask APIs. By defining roles, permissions, and mechanisms for assigning roles to users, you can ensure that users have access to the resources and actions that are necessary for their roles. Follow best practices for implementing RBAC, including granular permissions, role hierarchy, centralized role management, secure role assignment, error handling, regular auditing, and testing, to ensure the security and reliability of your Flask APIs.

Protecting Specific Resources and Endpoints

Protecting specific resources and endpoints is crucial for ensuring the security of Flask APIs. By restricting access to certain endpoints or resources, you can prevent unauthorized users from accessing sensitive data or performing privileged actions. Let's explore how to protect specific resources and endpoints in Flask APIs, along with code examples and best practices for Flask API development.

Introduction to Endpoint Protection

Protecting specific resources and endpoints involves implementing access control mechanisms to restrict access based on user roles, permissions, or authentication status. This ensures that only authorized users can access sensitive or privileged resources.

Implementing Endpoint Protection in Flask

There are several approaches to implementing endpoint protection in Flask APIs, including role-based access control (RBAC), token-based authentication, and custom decorators.

Example Code: Role-Based Access Control (RBAC)

```python
from flask import Flask, jsonify, request
from functools import wraps

app = Flask(__name__)

# Dummy user data (replace with actual user data)
users = {
    'john': {'password': 'password', 'roles': ['admin']},
    'jane': {'password': 'password123', 'roles': ['user']}
}
```

```python
# Dummy role permissions (replace with actual permissions)
role_permissions = {
    'admin': ['read', 'write', 'delete'],
    'user': ['read']
}

# Custom decorator to check permissions
def has_permission(permission):
    def decorator(func):
        @wraps(func)
        def wrapper(*args, **kwargs):
            user_roles = users.get(request.authorization.username).get('roles')
            if permission in role_permissions.get(user_roles[0]):
                return func(*args, **kwargs)
            else:
                return jsonify({"error": "Insufficient permissions"}), 403
        return wrapper
    return decorator

# Protected endpoint with permission check
@app.route('/protected')
@has_permission('read')
def protected_endpoint():
```

```
    return jsonify({"message": "Access granted"})

if __name__ == '__main__':
    app.run(debug=True)
```

In this example, we define a custom decorator `has_permission` that checks if the user has the required permission based on their assigned role. The `protected_endpoint` is a sample protected endpoint where access is granted only to users with the "read" permission.

Best Practices for Protecting Specific Resources and Endpoints

1. Granular Permissions: Define granular permissions to provide fine-grained control over user access to specific endpoints and resources.

2. Role-Based Access Control (RBAC): Implement RBAC to manage user roles, permissions, and access control policies effectively.

3. Authentication: Require authentication for accessing sensitive endpoints or resources to ensure that only authenticated users can access them.

4. Authorization Middleware: Implement authorization middleware to enforce access control policies across all endpoints and resources uniformly.

5. Error Handling: Provide informative error messages to users in case of permission errors or unauthorized access attempts to help them understand and troubleshoot the issue.

6. Regular Auditing: Regularly audit endpoint protection mechanisms and access control policies to ensure compliance with security requirements and identify potential vulnerabilities.

7. Testing: Thoroughly test endpoint protection mechanisms and access control policies to verify that only authorized users can access specific resources and endpoints.

Protecting specific resources and endpoints is essential for maintaining the security and integrity of Flask APIs. By implementing access control mechanisms such as role-based access control (RBAC), authentication, and custom decorators, you can restrict access to sensitive or privileged resources based on user roles, permissions, or authentication status. Follow best practices for protecting specific resources and endpoints, including granular permissions, RBAC, authentication, authorization middleware, error handling, regular auditing, and testing, to ensure the security and reliability of your Flask APIs.

Best Practices for Secure Authorization

Secure authorization is essential for ensuring that only authorized users have access to specific resources and endpoints in Flask APIs. Authorization involves determining whether a user has the necessary permissions to perform a certain action or access a particular resource. To implement secure authorization in Flask APIs, it's important to follow best practices and employ robust security measures. Let's explore these best practices along with code examples and recommendations for Flask API development.

1. Role-Based Access Control (RBAC)

Role-Based Access Control (RBAC) is a widely-used approach for managing user permissions and access control. In RBAC, users are assigned roles, and each role has specific permissions associated with it. By implementing RBAC, you can enforce fine-grained access control policies and ensure that users only have access to the resources and actions that are appropriate for their roles.

Example Code:

```python
from flask import Flask, jsonify, request
from functools import wraps

app = Flask(__name__)

# Dummy user data (replace with actual user data)
users = {
    'admin': {'password': 'admin', 'roles': ['admin']},
    'user': {'password': 'user', 'roles': ['user']}
}

# Dummy role permissions (replace with actual permissions)
role_permissions = {
    'admin': ['read', 'write', 'delete'],
    'user': ['read']
}

# Custom decorator to check permissions
def has_permission(permission):
    def decorator(func):
        @wraps(func)
        def wrapper(*args, **kwargs):
            user_roles = users.get(request.authorization.username).get('roles')
```

```
        if permission in
role_permissions.get(user_roles[0]):
            return func(*args, **kwargs)
        else:
            return jsonify({"error": "Insufficient
permissions"}), 403
    return wrapper
  return decorator

# Protected endpoint with permission check
@app.route('/protected')
@has_permission('read')
def protected_endpoint():
  return jsonify({"message": "Access granted"})

if __name__ == '__main__':
  app.run(debug=True)
```

2. Token-Based Authentication

Token-based authentication is a popular method for securing APIs by issuing tokens to authenticated users. These tokens are then sent with each request to access protected resources. By using token-based authentication, you can ensure secure communication between clients and servers without the need for session management.

Example Code:

```python
from flask import Flask, jsonify, request
from flask_jwt_extended import JWTManager, jwt_required, create_access_token, get_jwt_identity

app = Flask(__name__)
app.config['JWT_SECRET_KEY'] = 'secret_key'
jwt = JWTManager(app)

# Dummy user data (replace with actual user data)
users = {
    'admin': 'admin',
    'user': 'user'
}

@app.route('/login', methods=['POST'])
def login():
    data = request.json
    username = data.get('username')
    password = data.get('password')
    if username in users and users[username] == password:
        access_token = create_access_token(identity=username)
        return jsonify(access_token=access_token)
```

```
    else:
        return jsonify({"error": "Invalid username or password"}), 401

@app.route('/protected')
@jwt_required()
def protected_endpoint():
    current_user = get_jwt_identity()
    return jsonify({"message": "Access granted for {}".format(current_user)})

if __name__ == '__main__':
    app.run(debug=True)
```

3. Secure Communication (HTTPS)

Always use HTTPS to encrypt communication between clients and servers. HTTPS ensures that data transmitted over the network is secure and protected from eavesdropping and tampering. By using HTTPS, you can safeguard sensitive information such as authentication tokens and user credentials.

4. Input Validation and Sanitization

Perform input validation and sanitization to prevent injection attacks and ensure data integrity. Validate and sanitize user inputs before processing them to mitigate the risk of SQL injection, XSS (Cross-Site Scripting), and other security vulnerabilities.

5. Error Handling

Implement proper error handling mechanisms to handle authorization errors gracefully. Provide informative error messages to users in case of unauthorized access attempts or permission errors. This helps users understand the reason for the error and how to resolve it.

6. Rate Limiting

Apply rate limiting to prevent brute-force attacks and protect against DoS (Denial of Service) attacks. Limit the number of requests allowed from a single IP address or user within a certain time frame to mitigate the risk of unauthorized access attempts and ensure the availability of resources.

7. Regular Security Audits

Regularly audit your authorization mechanisms and access control policies to identify potential vulnerabilities and security weaknesses. Conduct security assessments and penetration testing to assess the effectiveness of your security measures and identify areas for improvement.

Secure authorization is essential for ensuring the security and integrity of Flask APIs. By following best practices such as role-based access control (RBAC), token-based authentication, secure communication (HTTPS), input validation and sanitization, error handling, rate limiting, and regular security audits, you can effectively protect your APIs against unauthorized access and security threats. Implementing robust authorization mechanisms helps safeguard sensitive data and resources, providing users with a secure and reliable experience.

Chapter 7

Unit Testing: Isolating and Validating Individual Components

Unit testing is a crucial aspect of Flask API development, as it allows developers to isolate and validate individual components of their application to ensure they function correctly. By writing unit tests, developers can identify bugs early in the development process, maintain code quality, and increase confidence in the reliability of their APIs. Let's explore the importance of unit testing in Flask API development, along with code examples and best practices for writing effective unit tests.

Importance of Unit Testing in Flask API Development

Unit testing is essential for Flask API development for several reasons:

1. Identifying Bugs Early: Unit tests help identify bugs and issues in individual components of the API early in the development process, making it easier to fix them before they escalate into larger problems.

2. Maintaining Code Quality: Unit tests serve as documentation for the behavior of individual components, making it easier for developers to understand and maintain the codebase over time.

3. Ensuring Reliability: Unit tests provide assurance that individual components of the API work as expected, increasing confidence in the reliability and stability of the application.

4. Supporting Refactoring: Unit tests allow developers to refactor code with confidence, knowing that any changes made will not introduce unexpected behavior or regressions.

Writing Unit Tests in Flask

Flask applications can be tested using the built-in `unittest` module or third-party testing frameworks like `pytest`. Unit tests typically focus on testing individual functions, routes, or components of the API in isolation.

Example Code using `unittest`

```python
import unittest
from myapp import app
```

```python
class TestApp(unittest.TestCase):

    def setUp(self):
        app.config['TESTING'] = True
        self.app = app.test_client()

    def test_home_route(self):
        response = self.app.get('/')
        self.assertEqual(response.status_code, 200)
        self.assertIn(b'Hello, World!', response.data)

    def test_add_route(self):
        response = self.app.post('/add', json={'a': 2, 'b': 3})
        self.assertEqual(response.status_code, 200)
        self.assertEqual(response.json['result'], 5)

if __name__ == '__main__':
    unittest.main()
```

In this example, we use the `unittest.TestCase` class to define test cases for the Flask API. We set up a test client using `app.test_client()` to simulate HTTP requests, and then define test methods to validate the behavior of different routes or endpoints.

Example Code using `pytest`

```python
import pytest
from myapp import app

@pytest.fixture
def client():
    app.config['TESTING'] = True
    with app.test_client() as client:
        yield client

def test_home_route(client):
    response = client.get('/')
    assert response.status_code == 200
    assert b'Hello, World!' in response.data

def test_add_route(client):
    response = client.post('/add', json={'a': 2, 'b': 3})
    assert response.status_code == 200
    assert response.json['result'] == 5
```

In this example, we use `pytest` as the testing framework. We define a fixture `client` to set up the test client, and then write test functions to validate the behavior of different routes or endpoints.

Best Practices for Writing Unit Tests in Flask

1. Isolate Test Cases: Ensure that each test case is independent and does not rely on the state or output of other test cases.

2. Use Mocking: Mock external dependencies or services to isolate the component being tested and ensure that tests are deterministic.

3. Test Edge Cases: Write test cases to cover edge cases, boundary conditions, and error scenarios to ensure robustness and reliability.

4. Keep Tests Fast and Lightweight: Write tests that execute quickly and do not have unnecessary dependencies or setup.

5. Use Descriptive Test Names: Use descriptive and meaningful names for test cases to clearly convey their purpose and intention.

6. Test Coverage: Aim for high test coverage to ensure that all critical paths and functionality of the API are tested.

7. Continuous Integration: Integrate unit tests into your CI/CD pipeline to automatically run tests on each code commit and detect regressions early.

Unit testing is an essential practice in Flask API development for ensuring the reliability, maintainability, and quality of the codebase. By writing unit tests, developers can identify and fix bugs early in the development process, maintain code quality, and increase confidence in the reliability of their APIs. Follow best practices for writing effective unit tests, such as isolating test cases, using mocking, testing edge cases, keeping tests fast and lightweight, using descriptive test names, aiming for high test coverage, and integrating tests into CI/CD pipelines, to ensure the success of your Flask API projects.

Integration Testing: Ensuring Different Parts of Your API Work Together Seamlessly

Integration testing is a critical aspect of Flask API development, as it ensures that different parts of the API work together seamlessly. Integration tests validate the interactions between various components of the API, including routes, middleware, databases, and external services, to verify that the system as a whole behaves as expected. Let's explore the importance of integration testing in Flask API development, along with code examples and best practices for writing effective integration tests.

Importance of Integration Testing in Flask API Development

Integration testing plays a crucial role in Flask API development for several reasons:

1. Validating Interactions: Integration tests validate the interactions between different components of the API, including routes, middleware, databases, and external services, to ensure they work together correctly.

2. Detecting Integration Issues: Integration tests help detect integration issues, such as compatibility problems between components or unexpected behavior resulting from interactions between different parts of the API.

3. Verifying End-to-End Functionality: Integration tests verify the end-to-end functionality of the API, ensuring that it behaves as expected from the perspective of the user or client.

4. Identifying Performance Bottlenecks: Integration tests can help identify performance bottlenecks or scalability issues resulting from interactions between components, allowing developers to optimize the API's performance.

Writing Integration Tests in Flask

Integration tests in Flask typically involve testing the API's behavior by making HTTP requests to various endpoints and verifying the responses. These tests can cover scenarios such as user authentication, data retrieval, data manipulation, error handling, and interactions with external services.

Example Code using `unittest`

```python
import unittest
from myapp import app, db

class TestIntegration(unittest.TestCase):

    def setUp(self):
        app.config['TESTING'] = True
        app.config['SQLALCHEMY_DATABASE_URI'] = 'sqlite:///:memory:'
        self.app = app.test_client()
        db.create_all()

    def tearDown(self):
        db.session.remove()
        db.drop_all()

    def test_get_users(self):
```

```
        response = self.app.get('/users')
        self.assertEqual(response.status_code, 200)
        self.assertIn(b'John', response.data)

    def test_add_user(self):
        response = self.app.post('/users', json={'name': 'Jane', 'email': 'jane@example.com'})
        self.assertEqual(response.status_code, 201)
        self.assertIn(b'Jane', response.data)
```

In this example, we use the `unittest.TestCase` class to define integration test cases for the Flask API. We set up a test client using `app.test_client()` and define test methods to validate the behavior of different endpoints.

Example Code using `pytest`

```python
import pytest
from myapp import app, db

@pytest.fixture
def client():
    app.config['TESTING'] = True
    app.config['SQLALCHEMY_DATABASE_URI'] = 'sqlite:///:memory:'
    with app.test_client() as client:
```

```
        db.create_all()
        yield client
        db.session.remove()
        db.drop_all()

def test_get_users(client):
    response = client.get('/users')
    assert response.status_code == 200
    assert b'John' in response.data

def test_add_user(client):
    response = client.post('/users', json={'name': 'Jane', 'email': 'jane@example.com'})
    assert response.status_code == 201
    assert b'Jane' in response.data
```

In this example, we use `pytest` as the testing framework. We define a fixture `client` to set up the test client, create a temporary in-memory SQLite database, and then write test functions to validate the behavior of different endpoints.

Best Practices for Writing Integration Tests in Flask

1. Isolate Test Environment: Set up a clean and isolated test environment for each integration test to prevent interference between tests.

2. Use Temporary Databases: Use temporary or in-memory databases for integration tests to avoid altering the state of production databases and ensure repeatability.

3. Test Realistic Scenarios: Write integration tests that cover realistic scenarios and use cases to verify the API's behavior in real-world situations.

4. Mock External Dependencies: Mock external services or dependencies that are not under test control to isolate the component being tested and ensure determinism.

5. Test Data Management: Manage test data carefully to ensure consistency and reliability across integration tests. Use fixtures or factories to create test data programmatically.

6. Monitor Test Coverage: Monitor test coverage and aim for high coverage to ensure that critical paths and functionality of the API are tested.

7. Continuous Integration: Integrate integration tests into your CI/CD pipeline to automatically run tests on each code commit and detect integration issues early.

Integration testing is essential for ensuring the reliability, compatibility, and functionality of Flask APIs. By writing integration tests, developers can validate the interactions between different components of the API and verify that they work together seamlessly. Follow best practices for writing effective integration tests, such as isolating the test environment, using temporary databases, testing realistic scenarios, mocking external dependencies, managing test data carefully, monitoring test coverage, and integrating tests into CI/CD pipelines, to ensure the success of your Flask API projects.

Test-Driven Development (TDD): A Proactive Approach to Building Robust APIs

Test-Driven Development (TDD) is a proactive approach to building robust APIs in Flask. It emphasizes writing tests before writing the actual code, ensuring that the code meets the desired requirements and behaves as expected. TDD promotes better code quality, faster development cycles, and increased confidence in the reliability of the API. Let's explore the principles of TDD in Flask API development, along with code examples and best practices for implementing TDD effectively.

Principles of Test-Driven Development (TDD)

TDD follows a simple cycle known as the "Red-Green-Refactor" cycle:

1. Red: Write a failing test that defines the desired behavior or functionality.

2. Green: Write the minimum amount of code necessary to make the test pass.

3. Refactor: Refactor the code to improve readability, maintainability, and efficiency while ensuring that all tests still pass.

Benefits of Test-Driven Development (TDD)

1. Improved Code Quality: TDD encourages writing clean, modular, and maintainable code by focusing on requirements and functionality from the outset.

2. Faster Development Cycles: TDD speeds up development cycles by providing immediate feedback on code changes and reducing the time spent debugging and fixing issues later in the development process.

3. Reduced Risk of Bugs: TDD helps identify bugs early in the development process, making it easier and less costly to fix them before they escalate into larger problems.

4. Increased Confidence: TDD increases confidence in the reliability and correctness of the codebase by ensuring that all functionality is thoroughly tested and verified.

Implementing Test-Driven Development (TDD) in Flask

Let's walk through an example of implementing TDD in Flask API development using the "Red-Green-Refactor" cycle.

Step 1: Write a Failing Test

```python
# test_users.py

import unittest
from myapp import app, db

class TestUsers(unittest.TestCase):

    def setUp(self):
        app.config['TESTING'] = True
        app.config['SQLALCHEMY_DATABASE_URI'] = 'sqlite:///:memory:'
        self.app = app.test_client()
```

```
        db.create_all()

    def tearDown(self):
        db.session.remove()
        db.drop_all()

    def test_get_users(self):
        response = self.app.get('/users')
        self.assertEqual(response.status_code, 200)
        self.assertIn(b'John', response.data)

if __name__ == '__main__':
    unittest.main()
```

Step 2: Write Code to Make the Test Pass

```python
# myapp.py

from flask import Flask, jsonify

app = Flask(__name__)

@app.route('/users')
def get_users():
    users = ['John', 'Jane', 'Doe']
    return jsonify(users)
```

```
if __name__ == '__main__':
    app.run(debug=True)
```

Step 3: Refactor the Code

```python
# myapp.py

from flask import Flask, jsonify

app = Flask(__name__)

@app.route('/users')
def get_users():
    users = ['John', 'Jane', 'Doe']
    return jsonify(users)

if __name__ == '__main__':
    app.run(debug=True)
```

Best Practices for Test-Driven Development (TDD) in Flask

1. Start Small: Begin with simple, granular tests that focus on individual components or functions before moving on to more complex tests.

2. Write Minimal Code: Write the minimum amount of code necessary to make the test pass, following the "YAGNI" (You Ain't Gonna Need It) principle.

3. Refactor Regularly: Refactor the code continuously to improve readability, maintainability, and efficiency while ensuring that all tests still pass.

4. Use Meaningful Test Names: Use descriptive and meaningful test names that clearly convey the intended behavior or functionality being tested.

5. Test Edge Cases and Error Scenarios: Write tests to cover edge cases, boundary conditions, and error scenarios to ensure robustness and reliability.

6. Maintain High Test Coverage: Aim for high test coverage to ensure that critical paths and functionality of the API are thoroughly tested and verified.

7. Integrate Tests into CI/CD Pipelines: Integrate tests into your CI/CD pipelines to automatically run tests on each code commit and detect issues early in the development process.

Test-Driven Development (TDD) is a proactive approach to building robust APIs in Flask that emphasizes writing tests before writing the actual code. By following the "Red-Green-Refactor" cycle, developers can ensure that the code meets the desired requirements and behaves as expected. TDD promotes better code quality, faster development cycles, and increased confidence in the reliability of the API. Follow best practices for implementing TDD effectively, such as starting small, writing minimal code, refactoring regularly, using meaningful test names, testing edge cases and error scenarios, maintaining high test coverage, and integrating tests into CI/CD pipelines, to ensure the success of your Flask API projects.

Popular Testing Frameworks for Flask: Unittest, pytest, and More

Testing frameworks are essential tools for writing and running tests in Flask applications. They provide a structured and organized way to create, execute, and manage tests, ensuring the reliability and quality of Flask APIs. In this article, we'll explore some of the popular testing frameworks for Flask, including `unittest`, `pytest`, and others. We'll also provide code examples and best practices for using these frameworks in Flask API development.

1. Unittest

`unittest` is a built-in testing framework in Python that provides a comprehensive set of tools for writing and executing unit tests. It follows the xUnit style of testing and offers features such as test discovery, fixtures, assertions, and test runners.

Example Code:

```python
import unittest
from myapp import app

class TestApp(unittest.TestCase):

    def setUp(self):
        app.config['TESTING'] = True
        self.app = app.test_client()

    def test_home_route(self):
        response = self.app.get('/')
        self.assertEqual(response.status_code, 200)
        self.assertIn(b'Hello, World!', response.data)

if __name__ == '__main__':
    unittest.main()
```

```

## 2. pytest

`pytest` is a popular testing framework for Python that provides a simpler and more flexible alternative to `unittest`. It offers features such as fixtures, parameterized testing, test discovery, and powerful assertions, making it a favorite among Python developers.

**Example Code:**

```python
import pytest
from myapp import app

@pytest.fixture
def client():
    app.config['TESTING'] = True
    with app.test_client() as client:
        yield client

def test_home_route(client):
    response = client.get('/')
    assert response.status_code == 200
    assert b'Hello, World!' in response.data
```
```

3. Flask-Testing

`Flask-Testing` is an extension for Flask that provides additional utilities and tools for testing Flask applications. It simplifies common testing tasks such as creating test clients, managing application contexts, and interacting with Flask extensions.

Example Code:

```python
from flask_testing import TestCase
from myapp import app

class TestApp(TestCase):

    def create_app(self):
        app.config['TESTING'] = True
        return app

    def test_home_route(self):
        response = self.client.get('/')
        self.assert200(response)
        self.assertContains(response, 'Hello, World!')
```

Best Practices for Testing in Flask

1. Isolate Test Environment: Set up a clean and isolated test environment for each test to prevent interference between tests.

2. Use Mocking: Mock external dependencies or services that are not under test control to isolate the component being tested.

3. Test Coverage: Aim for high test coverage to ensure that critical paths and functionality of the API are thoroughly tested and verified.

4. Parameterized Testing: Use parameterized testing to test a function with multiple inputs and expected outputs, reducing code duplication.

5. Test Driven Development (TDD): Follow the TDD approach by writing tests before writing the actual code to ensure code correctness and functionality.

6. Continuous Integration (CI): Integrate tests into your CI/CD pipelines to automatically run tests on each code commit and detect issues early in the development process.

7. Documentation: Document test cases and their expected behavior to make it easier for developers to understand and maintain the tests.

Testing frameworks play a crucial role in Flask API development by providing a structured and organized way to create, execute, and manage tests. `unittest`, `pytest`, and `Flask-Testing` are popular choices for testing Flask applications, each offering its own set of features and benefits. By following best practices for testing in Flask, such as isolating test environments, using mocking, aiming for high test coverage, practicing TDD, integrating tests into CI/CD pipelines, and documenting test cases, developers can ensure the reliability, quality, and success of their Flask API projects.

Chapter 8

Setting Up a Local Development Server for Testing and Iteration

Setting up a local development server for testing and iteration is essential for Flask API development, as it allows developers to test their code in a controlled environment before deploying it to production. In this article, we'll explore the steps for setting up a local development server for Flask APIs, along with code examples and best practices for efficient testing and iteration.

Setting Up a Local Development Server

To set up a local development server for testing and iteration in Flask, follow these steps:

Step 1: Install Flask

First, make sure you have Flask installed. You can install it using pip:

```
pip install Flask
```

Step 2: Create a Flask Application

Create a new directory for your Flask application and create a Python file for your Flask app. Here's a simple example:

```python
# app.py

from flask import Flask

app = Flask(__name__)

@app.route('/')
def hello():
    return 'Hello, World!'

if __name__ == '__main__':
    app.run(debug=True)
```

Step 3: Run the Flask Application

Run the Flask application using the `flask run` command:

```
export FLASK_APP=app.py
```

```
export FLASK_ENV=development
flask run
```

Best Practices for Local Development Servers

1. Use Environment Variables: Use environment variables to configure your Flask application, such as setting the Flask app and environment variables.

2. Debug Mode: Enable debug mode (`debug=True`) in the Flask application during development to automatically reload the server when code changes are detected and to display detailed error messages.

3. Virtual Environments: Use virtual environments to isolate dependencies for each project and avoid conflicts between packages.

4. Database Setup: Set up a local database for testing and development purposes, such as SQLite, PostgreSQL, or MySQL, and configure your Flask application to use it.

5. Logging: Use logging to track application behavior and debug issues during development.

6. Testing Endpoints: Test endpoints using tools like `curl`, `Postman`, or browser extensions to verify their behavior and response.

7. Code Version Control: Use version control systems like Git to track changes to your codebase and collaborate with other developers.

Example: Advanced Local Development Setup

In a more advanced setup, you can use Flask blueprints for modular application structure and Flask extensions for additional functionality. Here's an example:

```python
# app.py

from flask import Flask
from flask_sqlalchemy import SQLAlchemy

app = Flask(__name__)
app.config['SQLALCHEMY_DATABASE_URI'] = 'sqlite:///database.db'
app.config['SQLALCHEMY_TRACK_MODIFICATIONS'] = False
app.config['SECRET_KEY'] = 'secret'

db = SQLAlchemy(app)
```

```
# Import blueprints and register them
from auth.views import auth_blueprint
from users.views import users_blueprint

app.register_blueprint(auth_blueprint)
app.register_blueprint(users_blueprint)

if __name__ == '__main__':
    db.create_all()
    app.run(debug=True)
```
```

In this example, we set up a Flask application with SQLAlchemy for database integration. We also use Flask blueprints to organize routes into separate modules (`auth` and `users`). This modular approach makes the codebase more maintainable and scalable.

Setting up a local development server for testing and iteration is crucial for Flask API development. By following best practices such as using environment variables, enabling debug mode, using virtual environments, setting up a local database, logging, testing endpoints, and using advanced setups with Flask blueprints and extensions, developers can streamline the development process and ensure the reliability and quality of their Flask APIs. With a robust local
```

development server, developers can iterate quickly, debug issues efficiently, and deliver high-quality Flask APIs.

Deployment Options: Cloud Platforms like Heroku and AWS

Deploying a Flask API to a cloud platform like Heroku or AWS is a crucial step in making your API accessible to users over the internet. These platforms offer scalable infrastructure, easy deployment processes, and various services to support Flask applications. In this article, we'll explore deployment options for Flask APIs on Heroku and AWS, along with code examples and best practices for smooth deployment.

Heroku Deployment

Step 1: Set Up a Heroku Account

Sign up for a free account on Heroku if you haven't already done so.

Step 2: Install Heroku CLI

Install the Heroku Command Line Interface (CLI) to manage your Heroku apps from the terminal.

```
brew tap heroku/brew && brew install heroku
```

Step 3: Prepare Your Flask Application

Ensure your Flask application is ready for deployment. You may need to update configurations for production, such as database settings, environment variables, and security settings.

Step 4: Create a `Procfile`

Create a `Procfile` in the root directory of your project to specify how Heroku should run your application.

```
web: gunicorn app:app
```

Step 5: Initialize a Git Repository

Initialize a Git repository in your project directory if you haven't already done so.

```
git init
```

Step 6: Commit Your Changes

Commit your changes to the Git repository.

```
git add .
git commit -m "Initial commit"
```

Step 7: Create a Heroku App

Create a new Heroku app using the Heroku CLI.

```
heroku create <app-name>
```

Step 8: Deploy Your App

Deploy your app to Heroku.

```
git push heroku master
```

Step 9: Scale Your App

Scale your app by specifying the number of dynos (containers) to run.

```
heroku ps:scale web=1
```

Step 10: Access Your App

Your Flask app is now deployed to Heroku. You can access it using the provided URL.

```
heroku open
```

AWS Deployment

Step 1: Set Up an AWS Account

Sign up for an AWS account if you haven't already done so.

Step 2: Configure AWS CLI

Install and configure the AWS Command Line Interface (CLI) to interact with AWS services from the terminal.

```
pip install awscli
aws configure
```

Step 3: Prepare Your Flask Application

Ensure your Flask application is ready for deployment. Update configurations for production, such as database settings, environment variables, and security settings.

Step 4: Package Your Application

Package your Flask application into a ZIP file along with any dependencies.

```
pip install -r requirements.txt -t .
zip -r app.zip ./*
```

Step 5: Upload Your Application to S3

Upload your packaged application to an S3 bucket.

```
aws s3 cp app.zip s3://<bucket-name>/
```

Step 6: Create an Elastic Beanstalk Application

Create a new Elastic Beanstalk application using the AWS Management Console or the CLI.

```
aws elasticbeanstalk create-application --application-name <app-name>
```

Step 7: Create an Environment

Create an environment for your Elastic Beanstalk application.

```
aws elasticbeanstalk create-environment --application-name <app-name> --environment-name <env-name> --solution-stack-name "64bit Amazon Linux 2 v3.3.2 running Python 3.8"
```

Step 8: Deploy Your Application

Deploy your application to the Elastic Beanstalk environment.

```
aws elasticbeanstalk create-deployment --application-name <app-name> --environment-name <env-name> --version-label v1 --source-bundle S3Bucket=<bucket-name>,S3Key=app.zip
```

Step 9: Access Your Application

Your Flask app is now deployed to AWS Elastic Beanstalk. You can access it using the provided URL.

Best Practices for Deployment

1. Environment Configuration: Use environment variables to manage sensitive information such as API keys, database credentials, and secret keys.

2. Automated Deployment: Set up continuous integration and deployment (CI/CD) pipelines to automate the deployment process and ensure consistent deployments.

3. Monitoring and Logging: Monitor your deployed application using tools like CloudWatch (AWS) or Papertrail (Heroku) and set up logging to track errors and performance metrics.

4. Scaling: Configure auto-scaling to automatically adjust the number of instances based on traffic demand and ensure optimal performance.

5. Security: Implement security best practices such as HTTPS, encryption, firewalls, and access controls to protect your application and data from unauthorized access and attacks.

6. Backup and Disaster Recovery: Regularly back up your application data and implement disaster recovery plans to mitigate the risk of data loss and ensure business continuity.

Deploying a Flask API to a cloud platform like Heroku or AWS is a straightforward process, but it requires careful planning and configuration to ensure a smooth deployment. By following best practices such as environment configuration, automated deployment, monitoring and logging, scaling, security, and backup and disaster recovery, you can deploy your Flask API with confidence and ensure its reliability, scalability, and security in production. With your Flask API deployed to the cloud, you can make it accessible to users over the internet and provide valuable services to your users and customers.

Configuration Management for Production Environments

Configuration management for production environments is crucial for Flask API development to ensure that your application runs smoothly and securely in a production setting. By managing configurations properly, you can separate environment-specific settings from your application code, making it easier to deploy, maintain, and scale your Flask API. In this article, we'll explore best practices for configuration management in Flask, along with code examples and strategies for handling configurations in production environments.

Importance of Configuration Management

Effective configuration management in Flask API development offers several benefits:

1. Security: Keeping sensitive information such as database credentials, API keys, and secret keys separate from your code reduces the risk of exposure and unauthorized access.

2. Portability: Storing environment-specific configurations separately allows you to easily deploy your Flask application across different environments (development, staging, production) without modifying the code.

3. Maintainability: Centralized configuration management makes it easier to update settings and parameters across multiple instances of your Flask application.

4. Scalability: Configuration management practices enable you to scale your application horizontally by spinning up additional instances with consistent configurations.

Best Practices for Configuration Management in Flask

1. Use Environment Variables

Store environment-specific configurations such as database URLs, API keys, and secret keys as environment variables. Flask provides a built-in mechanism for accessing environment variables using `os.environ`.

```python
import os

SECRET_KEY = os.environ.get('SECRET_KEY')
```

```
SQLALCHEMY_DATABASE_URI =
os.environ.get('DATABASE_URL')
```

2. Configuration Files

Store environment-specific configurations in separate configuration files (e.g., `config.py`, `config_dev.py`, `config_prod.py`). Use the `app.config.from_object()` method to load configurations from these files based on the environment.

```python
# config_dev.py
DEBUG = True
SQLALCHEMY_DATABASE_URI = 'sqlite:///dev.db'

# config_prod.py
DEBUG = False
SQLALCHEMY_DATABASE_URI = 'postgresql://user:password@localhost/db_name'
```

3. Environment Detection

Detects the environment automatically based on predefined conditions such as the presence of environment variables or command-line arguments. This allows your Flask application to adapt its behavior dynamically.

```python
import os

if 'DATABASE_URL' in os.environ:
    app.config.from_object('config_prod')
else:
    app.config.from_object('config_dev')
```

4. Secret Management

Use secure and robust solutions for managing sensitive information such as secret keys and API keys. Avoid hardcoding secrets in code or configuration files and consider using dedicated secret management tools or services.

```python
# Use environment variables for secret keys
SECRET_KEY = os.environ.get('SECRET_KEY')
```

5. Encrypted Configurations

Encrypt sensitive configuration files to protect them from unauthorized access. Use tools like `git-crypt` or encryption libraries to encrypt configuration files before committing them to version control.

6. Testing Configurations

Test your configurations thoroughly in different environments (development, staging, production) to ensure that they behave as expected and meet the requirements of each environment.

Example: Dynamic Configuration Loading

```python
import os
from flask import Flask

app = Flask(__name__)

if 'DATABASE_URL' in os.environ:
    app.config.from_object('config_prod')
else:
    app.config.from_object('config_dev')

@app.route('/')
def hello():
    return 'Hello, World!'
```

```
if __name__ == '__main__':
    app.run()
```

Configuration management is a critical aspect of Flask API development, especially in production environments. By following best practices such as using environment variables, configuration files, environment detection, secret management, encrypted configurations, and testing configurations, you can ensure that your Flask application runs smoothly, securely, and efficiently in production. With proper configuration management, you can separate environment-specific settings from your code, making it easier to deploy, maintain, and scale your Flask API across different environments. By adopting these best practices, you can build robust and reliable Flask APIs that meet the requirements of production environments and provide value to your users and customers.

Monitoring and Logging: Keeping an Eye on Your Deployed API

Monitoring and logging are essential aspects of Flask API development, especially in production environments, to ensure that your application runs smoothly, detect errors or issues, and troubleshoot performance bottlenecks effectively. By implementing robust monitoring and logging practices, you can gain insights into your deployed API's behavior, identify potential issues early, and maintain high availability and performance. In this article, we'll explore best practices for monitoring and logging in Flask, along with code examples and strategies for keeping an eye on your deployed API.

Importance of Monitoring and Logging

Monitoring and logging serve several critical purposes in Flask API development:

1. Error Detection: Monitoring and logging help detect errors, exceptions, and unexpected behavior in your API, allowing you to address issues promptly and prevent downtime.

2. Performance Monitoring: Monitoring metrics such as response time, throughput, and resource utilization helps identify performance bottlenecks and optimize the performance of your API.

3. Security: Monitoring and logging can help detect and respond to security incidents, such as unauthorized access attempts or suspicious activity, to protect your API and its data.

4. Compliance: Logging can be crucial for compliance with regulatory requirements and standards, such as GDPR or HIPAA, by providing an audit trail of API activity and data access.

Best Practices for Monitoring and Logging in Flask

1. Use a Logging Framework

Utilize a logging framework such as Python's built-in `logging` module or popular third-party libraries like `Loguru` or `structlog` to manage logging in your Flask application. Configure loggers, handlers, and formatters to control logging behavior and output formats.

```python
import logging

app = Flask(__name__)

# Configure logging
app.logger.setLevel(logging.INFO)
handler = logging.StreamHandler()
handler.setFormatter(logging.Formatter('%(asctime)s - %(name)s - %(levelname)s - %(message)s'))
app.logger.addHandler(handler)
```

2. Log Critical Information

Log critical information such as request details, error messages, stack traces, and database queries to provide context for troubleshooting issues and understanding the behavior of your API in production.

```python
@app.route('/example')
def example():
    try:
        # Business logic
        return jsonify({'message': 'Success'})
    except Exception as e:
        app.logger.error(f'An error occurred: {str(e)}', exc_info=True)
        return jsonify({'error': 'Internal Server Error'}), 500
```

3. Log Levels

Use different log levels (e.g., DEBUG, INFO, WARNING, ERROR, CRITICAL) to categorize log messages based on their severity. Adjust log levels dynamically based on the environment (e.g., development, staging, production) to control the verbosity of logging output.

```python
app.logger.setLevel(logging.INFO)
```

4. Centralized Logging

Aggregate and centralize logs from multiple instances of your Flask application using logging services or platforms such as AWS CloudWatch, Google Cloud Logging, or centralized logging solutions like ELK (Elasticsearch, Logstash, Kibana).

5. Monitoring Metrics

Collect and monitor key performance metrics such as response time, request throughput, error rate, CPU utilization, memory usage, and database performance using monitoring tools and services like Prometheus, Grafana, or New Relic.

6. Health Checks

Implement health checks endpoints in your Flask application to monitor the health and availability of your API. Health checks can verify essential components such as database connections, external dependencies, and system resources.

```python
@app.route('/health')
def health_check():
    return jsonify({'status': 'ok'})
```

7. Alerting

Configure alerts and notifications to be notified immediately when critical issues or anomalies are detected in your API. Set up alerting rules based on predefined thresholds or conditions using monitoring tools or services.

8. Continuous Improvement

Regularly review and analyze logs and monitoring data to identify trends, patterns, and areas for improvement in your Flask API. Use insights from monitoring and logging to optimize performance, enhance reliability, and prioritize development efforts.

Example: Logging Configuration in Flask

```python
import logging
from flask import Flask, jsonify
```

```
app = Flask(__name__)

# Configure logging
app.logger.setLevel(logging.INFO)
handler = logging.StreamHandler()
handler.setFormatter(logging.Formatter('%(asctime)s - %(name)s - %(levelname)s - %(message)s'))
app.logger.addHandler(handler)

@app.route('/')
def index():
    app.logger.info('Request received')
    return jsonify({'message': 'Hello, World!'})

if __name__ == '__main__':
    app.run()
```

Monitoring and logging are critical components of Flask API development that enable you to maintain visibility, troubleshoot issues, and optimize performance in production environments. By following best practices such as using a logging framework, logging critical information, adjusting log levels, centralizing logging, monitoring metrics, implementing health checks, configuring alerting, and continuously improving based on insights from monitoring and logging, you can ensure the reliability, availability, and performance of your Flask API. With effective monitoring and logging practices in place, you can proactively identify and address issues, deliver a seamless user experience, and meet the demands of your users and customers with confidence.

Chapter 9

Clean Coding Principles: Writing Code You (and Others) Can Love

Readability and Maintainability: Keeping Your Code Clean and Clear

Clean coding principles are essential in Flask API development to ensure that your code is easy to understand, maintain, and extend. By following best practices for readability and maintainability, you can create code that you (and others) can love, making it easier to collaborate, debug, and evolve your Flask API over time. In this article, we'll explore clean coding principles in the context of Flask API development, along with code examples and strategies for writing clean and clear code.

Importance of Readability and Maintainability

Readability and maintainability are crucial aspects of clean coding in Flask API development for several reasons:

1. Understanding: Readable code is easier to understand, reducing the time and effort required for developers to comprehend its purpose, functionality, and behavior.

2. Collaboration: Clear and well-organized code facilitates collaboration among team members, allowing developers to work together more effectively and efficiently.

3. Debugging: Readable code simplifies the debugging process by making it easier to identify and locate issues, errors, and inconsistencies in the codebase.

4. Refactoring: Maintainable code is easier to refactor and improve over time, enabling developers to evolve the codebase and address changing requirements or design patterns.

Best Practices for Readability and Maintainability in Flask API Development

1. Consistent Naming Conventions

Use consistent and descriptive names for variables, functions, classes, and routes in your Flask API. Follow Python's naming conventions (PEP 8) and use meaningful names that convey the purpose and context of each component.

```python
# Good example
@app.route('/users')
def get_users():
    pass

# Bad example
@app.route('/user_list')
def fetch_records():
    pass
```

2. Modularization and Separation of Concerns

Organize your Flask application into modular components such as blueprints, modules, and packages, and follow the principle of separation of concerns to keep related functionality grouped together and independent of each other.

```python
# Good example
# user_routes.py
from flask import Blueprint

user_blueprint = Blueprint('user', __name__)

@user_blueprint.route('/users')
```

```
def get_users():
    pass

# Bad example
# app.py
from flask import Flask

app = Flask(__name__)

@app.route('/users')
def get_users():
    pass
```

3. Proper Indentation and Formatting

Maintain consistent indentation and formatting throughout your codebase to improve readability and clarity. Use a consistent style guide and formatting tool (e.g., Black, Pylint) to enforce coding standards and conventions.

```python
# Good example
def process_data(data):
    for item in data:
        if item:
            print(item)
```

```python
# Bad example
def process_data(data):
    for item in data:
        if item:
            print(item)
```

4. Commenting and Documentation

Provide meaningful comments and docstrings to explain the purpose, functionality, and usage of your code. Document important functions, classes, and modules using descriptive docstrings to make them self-explanatory.

```python
# Good example
def calculate_total(items):
    """
    Calculate the total cost of items.

    Args:
        items (list): List of item prices.

    Returns:
        float: Total cost.
    """
```

```
    total = sum(items)
    return total

# Bad example
def total(items):
    # Calculate total
    total = sum(items)
    return total
```

5. Error Handling

Implement proper error handling and error messages to provide informative feedback to users and developers when errors occur. Use try-except blocks and custom error handlers to gracefully handle exceptions and prevent unexpected crashes.

```python
# Good example
@app.route('/user/<int:user_id>')
def get_user(user_id):
    try:
        user = User.query.get(user_id)
        if not user:
            return jsonify({'error': 'User not found'}), 404
        return jsonify(user.serialize())
    except Exception as e:
```

```
        app.logger.error(f'An error occurred: {str(e)}')
        return jsonify({'error': 'Internal Server Error'}), 500

# Bad example
@app.route('/user/<int:user_id>')
def get_user(user_id):
    user = User.query.get(user_id)
    return jsonify(user.serialize())
```

6. Test-Driven Development (TDD)

Follow the Test-Driven Development (TDD) approach by writing tests before writing the actual code. Use unit tests, integration tests, and end-to-end tests to ensure the correctness, functionality, and behavior of your Flask API.

```python
# Good example
import unittest
from myapp import app

class TestApp(unittest.TestCase):

    def setUp(self):
        app.config['TESTING'] = True
        self.app = app.test_client()
```

```python
    def test_home_route(self):
        response = self.app.get('/')
        self.assertEqual(response.status_code, 200)
        self.assertIn(b'Hello, World!', response.data)

if __name__ == '__main__':
    unittest.main()

# Bad example
import requests

def test_home_route():
    response = requests.get('http://localhost:5000/')
    assert response.status_code == 200
    assert 'Hello, World!' in response.text
```
```

## 7. Version Control

Use version control systems like Git to track changes to your codebase, collaborate with other developers, and maintain a history of revisions. Follow best practices for branching, committing, and merging to keep your codebase clean and organized.

Readability and maintainability are critical aspects of clean coding in Flask API development, enabling
```

developers to write code that is easy to understand, maintain, and extend. By following best practices such as consistent naming conventions, modularization, proper indentation and formatting, commenting and documentation, error handling, Test-Driven Development (TDD), and version control, you can create code that you (and others) can love. With clean and clear code, you can build robust, reliable, and scalable Flask APIs that meet the needs of your users and customers while facilitating collaboration, debugging, and evolution of your codebase over time.

Code Formatting and Linting: Enforcing Consistency and Style

Code formatting and linting are essential practices in Flask API development for enforcing consistency, style, and quality in your codebase. By adhering to consistent coding standards and best practices, you can improve readability, maintainability, and collaboration among developers, leading to cleaner, more reliable Flask APIs. In this article, we'll explore the importance of code formatting and linting in Flask development, along with code examples and strategies for enforcing consistency and style.

Importance of Code Formatting and Linting

Code formatting and linting serve several critical purposes in Flask API development:

1. Consistency: Enforcing consistent coding standards and styles across your codebase ensures that all developers follow the same conventions, making it easier to understand and maintain the code.

2. Readability: Properly formatted code is easier to read, understand, and navigate, reducing cognitive overhead and improving developer productivity.

3. Quality: Linting tools help identify and flag potential issues, errors, and violations of coding standards, allowing developers to address them proactively and maintain high-quality code.

4. Collaboration: Consistent formatting and linting practices facilitate collaboration among team members by providing a common set of guidelines and expectations for writing code.

Best Practices for Code Formatting and Linting in Flask API Development

1. Choose a Style Guide

Select a style guide or coding standard for your Flask API development, such as PEP 8 (Python Enhancement Proposal 8), and follow its recommendations for code formatting, naming conventions, and style.

2. Use a Linter

Integrate a linter such as Flake8, pylint, or Black into your development workflow to analyze your code for potential issues, errors, and violations of coding standards. Configure the linter to enforce specific rules and conventions according to your chosen style guide.

3. Automate Formatting and Linting

Automate code formatting and linting tasks using tools like Black, autopep8, or pylint, and integrate them into your development environment, IDE, or version control system to ensure consistency and enforce standards automatically.

4. Configure Editor Plugins

Configure editor plugins or extensions for your preferred text editor or IDE (e.g., Visual Studio Code, PyCharm) to provide real-time feedback, suggestions, and warnings based on code formatting and linting rules as you write code.

5. Enforce Pre-commit Hooks

Set up pre-commit hooks in your version control system (e.g., Git) to run code formatting and linting checks automatically before each commit, preventing non-compliant code from being committed to the repository.

6. Customize Linting Rules

Customize linting rules and configurations to tailor them to your specific project requirements and preferences. Adjust severity levels, ignore specific violations, or define custom rulesets as needed.

7. Regular Code Reviews

Conduct regular code reviews with team members to review code changes, provide feedback, and ensure adherence to coding standards and best practices. Use code review tools or platforms to facilitate collaboration and communication.

Example: Code Formatting and Linting in Flask API Development

```python
# Example using Flake8 and Black
```

```
# .flake8
[flake8]
max-line-length = 88
ignore = E203, E266, E501, W503
exclude = .git, __pycache__, .venv, .env, venv, env, .venv3, .tox, .eggs, *.egg

# .pre-commit-config.yaml
repos:
  - repo: https://github.com/pre-commit/pre-commit-hooks
    rev: v3.4.0
    hooks:
      - id: trailing-whitespace
      - id: end-of-file-fixer
      - id: check-yaml
      - id: check-added-large-files
  - repo: https://github.com/psf/black
    rev: 20.8b1
    hooks:
      - id: black
        language_version: python3
```

1. **Install Flake8 and Black:**

```bash
```

pip install flake8 black
```

## 2. Configure Flake8:

Create a `.flake8` configuration file in the root of your project to specify Flake8 settings and options.

## 3. Configure Pre-commit Hooks:

Create a `.pre-commit-config.yaml` file in the root of your project to define pre-commit hooks for code formatting and linting.

## 4. Run Pre-commit Hooks:

Run `pre-commit install` to install the pre-commit hooks and `pre-commit run --all-files` to run the hooks on all files in your repository.

Code formatting and linting are essential practices in Flask API development for enforcing consistency, style, and quality in your codebase. By following best practices such as choosing a style guide, using a linter, automating formatting and linting tasks, configuring editor plugins, enforcing pre-commit hooks, customizing linting rules, and conducting regular code reviews, you can ensure that your Flask APIs are clean, readable, and
```

maintainable. With consistent formatting and linting practices in place, you can improve collaboration, code quality, and developer productivity, leading to cleaner, more reliable Flask APIs that meet the needs of your users and customers.

Documentation: The User Manual for Your API

Documentation is the user manual for your Flask API, providing developers with essential information on how to interact with your API, including endpoints, parameters, request/response formats, authentication, and error handling. Well-written documentation is crucial for fostering adoption, enabling integration, and supporting developers in using your API effectively. In this article, we'll explore the importance of documentation in Flask API development, along with code examples and strategies for writing comprehensive and user-friendly documentation.

Importance of Documentation

Documentation plays a vital role in Flask API development for several reasons:

1. Onboarding: Documentation serves as a guide for developers who are new to your API, helping them understand its features, functionality, and usage.

2. Integration: Clear and concise documentation facilitates integration with your API by providing instructions on how to make requests, handle responses, and authenticate.

3. Support: Documentation acts as a reference for developers troubleshooting issues, debugging errors, and resolving challenges encountered while using your API.

4. Promotion: Well-documented APIs are more likely to be adopted by developers and organizations, as they instill confidence and trust in the reliability and usability of the API.

Best Practices for Documentation in Flask API Development

1. API Overview

Provide an overview of your Flask API, including its purpose, functionality, and key features. Describe the problem it solves and the value it offers to developers.

2. Getting Started

Offer a quick start guide to help developers get up and running with your API quickly. Include instructions for installing dependencies, setting up authentication, and making their first API requests.

3. Endpoint Reference

Document all endpoints exposed by your Flask API, including their URLs, HTTP methods, request parameters, and response formats. Use clear and descriptive names for endpoints and parameters to make them easy to understand.

4. Request/Response Examples

Provide examples of request payloads and response bodies for each endpoint to illustrate how to structure requests and interpret responses. Include sample code snippets in popular programming languages to demonstrate API usage.

5. Authentication

Explain the authentication mechanisms supported by your API, such as API keys, OAuth tokens, or JWT tokens. Describe how developers can obtain and use authentication credentials to access protected endpoints.

6. Error Handling

Document error codes, messages, and status responses returned by your API to indicate various error scenarios, such as invalid requests, authentication failures, or server errors. Include guidance on how to handle and troubleshoot errors.

7. Rate Limiting

Specify any rate limiting or throttling policies enforced by your API to manage API usage and prevent abuse. Provide details on rate limits, quotas, and rate limit headers included in API responses.

8. Versioning

If your API supports versioning, explain how versioning works and how developers can specify the API version in their requests. Include guidelines for handling deprecated endpoints and migrating to newer API versions.

Example: Documentation in Flask API Development

```python
from flask import Flask, jsonify
```

```
app = Flask(__name__)

@app.route('/hello')
def hello():
    """
    GET /hello

    Returns a friendly greeting message.

    Example:

    $ curl http://localhost:5000/hello

    Response:

    {
        "message": "Hello, World!"
    }
    """
    return jsonify({'message': 'Hello, World!'})

if __name__ == '__main__':
    app.run(debug=True)
```

Tools for Documentation

1. Swagger/OpenAPI

Use Swagger/OpenAPI specifications to define, document, and visualize your API endpoints, parameters, and responses. Swagger UI provides an interactive API documentation interface for testing and exploring your API.

2. Sphinx

Integrate Sphinx with Flask extensions like Flask-Sphinx-Themes or Flask-APIDoc to generate API documentation from docstrings and Markdown files. Sphinx supports customizing documentation themes, indexing, and cross-referencing.

3. Postman Collections

Export Postman collections containing requests, endpoints, and examples as API documentation. Postman provides features for organizing, sharing, and collaborating on API documentation within teams.

4. Redoc

Use Redoc to generate beautiful and interactive API documentation from OpenAPI/Swagger specifications.

Redoc offers customizable themes, responsive design, and support for rich text formatting and code samples.

Documentation is the user manual for your Flask API, providing developers with essential information on how to interact with your API effectively. By following best practices such as providing an API overview, offering a quick start guide, documenting endpoints, request/response examples, authentication, error handling, rate limiting, and versioning, you can create comprehensive and user-friendly documentation that promotes adoption, integration, and support of your API. With clear and concise documentation in place, you can empower developers to leverage the capabilities of your Flask API and build innovative applications that drive value for your users and customers.

Chapter 10

Flask-RESTful is a powerful extension for Flask that simplifies the process of building RESTful APIs by providing abstractions for common tasks such as routing, request parsing, serialization, and error handling. With Flask-RESTful, developers can streamline API development, improve code organization, and enhance scalability and maintainability. In this article, we'll explore Flask-RESTful and demonstrate how to use it to build RESTful APIs in Flask, following best practices and conventions.

Introduction to Flask-RESTful

Flask-RESTful extends Flask to provide additional functionality specifically designed for building RESTful APIs. It offers features such as request parsing, resource routing, response serialization, and error handling, allowing developers to focus on defining API endpoints and business logic without having to implement boilerplate code for common tasks.

Installation

You can install Flask-RESTful using pip:

```bash
pip install flask-restful
```

Basic Usage

Let's create a simple Flask application and define a RESTful API using Flask-RESTful:

```python
from flask import Flask
from flask_restful import Api, Resource

app = Flask(__name__)
api = Api(app)

class HelloWorld(Resource):
    def get(self):
        return {'message': 'Hello, World!'}

api.add_resource(HelloWorld, '/')

if __name__ == '__main__':
    app.run(debug=True)
```

In this example:

- We create a Flask application and instantiate the `Api` object from Flask-RESTful.

- We define a resource class `HelloWorld` that inherits from `Resource`.

- We define a GET method within the `HelloWorld` resource class that returns a simple JSON response.

- We register the `HelloWorld` resource with the API at the root URL `/`.

Now, when you run the Flask application and navigate to `http://localhost:5000/`, you should see the message "Hello, World!".

Creating Multiple Endpoints

You can define multiple endpoints by creating additional resource classes and registering them with the API:

```python
class GreetUser(Resource):
    def get(self, username):
        return {'message': f'Hello, {username}!'}

api.add_resource(GreetUser, '/greet/<string:username>')
```

```

In this example, we define a new resource class `GreetUser` with a GET method that takes a username parameter from the URL path. This endpoint responds with a personalized greeting message for the specified username.

**Request Parsing**

Flask-RESTful provides built-in support for parsing request data, including query parameters, form data, JSON payloads, and file uploads. You can use the `reqparse` module to define request parsers for extracting and validating request data:

```python
from flask_restful import reqparse

parser = reqparse.RequestParser()
parser.add_argument('name', type=str, required=True, help='Name is required')

class GreetUser(Resource):
    def get(self):
        args = parser.parse_args()
        name = args['name']
        return {'message': f'Hello, {name}!'}
```
```

```
api.add_resource(GreetUser, '/greet')
```

In this example, we define a request parser with a required `name` argument. The GET method of the `GreetUser` resource uses this parser to extract the `name` parameter from the request URL and respond with a personalized greeting message.

Serialization

Flask-RESTful simplifies the process of serializing response data by providing integration with popular serialization libraries such as Marshmallow. You can define schemas for your data models and use them to serialize objects into JSON responses:

```python
from flask_marshmallow import Marshmallow

ma = Marshmallow(app)

class UserSchema(ma.Schema):
    class Meta:
        fields = ('id', 'username', 'email')

user_schema = UserSchema()
```

```
class UserResource(Resource):
    def get(self, user_id):
        user = User.query.get(user_id)
        if not user:
            return {'message': 'User not found'}, 404
        return user_schema.dump(user)
```

In this example, we define a `UserSchema` using Marshmallow and use it to serialize `User` objects into JSON responses within the `UserResource` resource class.

Error Handling

Flask-RESTful provides built-in support for handling errors and exceptions in your API endpoints. You can define custom error handlers to handle specific error cases and return appropriate error responses:

```python
from flask_restful import abort

class UserResource(Resource):
    def get(self, user_id):
        user = User.query.get(user_id)
        if not user:
```

```
        abort(404, message='User not found')
    return user_schema.dump(user)
```

In this example, if the requested user does not exist, we use the `abort` function to abort the request and return a 404 error response with a custom error message.

Flask-RESTful is a powerful extension for Flask that simplifies the process of building RESTful APIs by providing abstractions for common tasks such as routing, request parsing, serialization, and error handling. By following best practices and conventions, you can use Flask-RESTful to streamline API development, improve code organization, and enhance scalability and maintainability. With Flask-RESTful, you can build robust and scalable RESTful APIs in Flask with ease, enabling you to focus on defining endpoints and business logic without having to implement boilerplate code for common tasks.

Marshmallow: Effortless Data Serialization and Validation

Marshmallow is a powerful library for serialization, validation, and deserialization of complex data structures in Python. It provides a simple and intuitive way to define schemas for your data models and convert them to and from native Python data types, making it effortless to work with data in Flask API development. In this article, we'll explore Marshmallow and demonstrate how to use it for data serialization and validation in Flask, following best practices and conventions.

Introduction to Marshmallow

Marshmallow is often used in Flask API development to handle the serialization and deserialization of data between Python objects and JSON representations. It provides a declarative way to define schemas for your data models, allowing you to specify the structure, fields, and validation rules for your data.

Installation

You can install Marshmallow using pip:

```bash
pip install marshmallow
```

Basic Usage

Let's start by creating a simple Marshmallow schema for a User object:

```python
from marshmallow import Schema, fields

class UserSchema(Schema):
    id = fields.Int(dump_only=True)
    username = fields.Str(required=True)
    email = fields.Email(required=True)
```

In this example:

- We define a `UserSchema` class that inherits from `Schema`.

- We define fields for the `id`, `username`, and `email` attributes of a User object.

- We specify that the `id` field is read-only (dump-only) and should not be included when serializing data.

Now, let's use the `UserSchema` to serialize and deserialize User objects:

```python
user_data = {
    'id': 1,
    'username': 'john_doe',
```

```
    'email': 'john.doe@example.com'
}

# Deserialize data to User object
user = UserSchema().load(user_data)

# Serialize User object to JSON
user_json = UserSchema().dump(user)
```

Data Validation

Marshmallow allows you to define validation rules for your fields to ensure that incoming data meets certain criteria:

```python
class UserSchema(Schema):
    id = fields.Int(dump_only=True)
    username = fields.Str(required=True, validate=Length(min=1, max=50))
    email = fields.Email(required=True)
```

In this example, we add validation rules to the `username` field to ensure that it is not empty and does not exceed 50 characters in length.

Nested Schemas

You can use nested schemas to represent relationships between different data models:

```python
class PostSchema(Schema):
    id = fields.Int(dump_only=True)
    title = fields.Str(required=True)
    body = fields.Str(required=True)
    author = fields.Nested(UserSchema)
```

In this example, we define a `PostSchema` with a nested `author` field representing a User object.

Custom Validation

You can define custom validation methods to perform complex validation logic:

```python
class UserSchema(Schema):
    id = fields.Int(dump_only=True)
    username = fields.Str(required=True)

    @validates('username')
    def validate_username(self, value):
```

```
       if len(value) < 3:
           raise ValidationError('Username must be at least 3 characters long.')
```

In this example, we define a custom validation method `validate_username` to ensure that the username is at least 3 characters long.

Integration with Flask

Marshmallow integrates seamlessly with Flask to handle data serialization and validation in Flask API development. You can use Marshmallow schemas within Flask routes to serialize/deserialize request data:

```python
from flask import Flask, request, jsonify
from marshmallow import ValidationError

app = Flask(__name__)

@app.route('/users', methods=['POST'])
def create_user():
    try:
        user_data = request.json
        user = UserSchema().load(user_data)
        # Save user to database
```

```
    return UserSchema().dump(user)
except ValidationError as e:
    return jsonify({'error': e.messages}), 400

if __name__ == '__main__':
    app.run(debug=True)
```

In this example, we define a Flask route to create a new user. We use the `UserSchema` to deserialize the request JSON data into a User object and handle any validation errors using Flask's error handling mechanism.

Marshmallow is a versatile library for serialization, validation, and deserialization of data in Flask API development. By defining schemas for your data models and leveraging Marshmallow's powerful features such as field validation, nested schemas, custom validation methods, and integration with Flask, you can effortlessly handle complex data structures and ensure data integrity and consistency in your Flask APIs. With Marshmallow, you can streamline the process of working with data, improve code organization, and enhance the robustness and scalability of your Flask applications.

Other Useful Extensions for Common Tasks

In Flask API development, there are several useful extensions available to streamline common tasks, enhance functionality, and improve productivity. These extensions cover a wide range of areas, including authentication, database integration, caching, testing, and more. In this article, we'll explore some of the most popular Flask extensions for common tasks, along with code examples and best practices for their usage.

Flask-CORS: Cross-Origin Resource Sharing

Flask-CORS is an extension that simplifies Cross-Origin Resource Sharing (CORS) in Flask applications, allowing you to specify which origins are allowed to access your API resources.

Installation:

```bash
pip install Flask-CORS
```

Usage:

```python
from flask import Flask
```

```
from flask_cors import CORS

app = Flask(__name__)
CORS(app)

@app.route('/')
def hello():
    return 'Hello, World!'
```

With Flask-CORS, you can easily configure CORS policies to control access to your API endpoints and prevent unauthorized cross-origin requests.

Flask-JWT-Extended: JSON Web Tokens

Flask-JWT-Extended is an extension that adds support for JSON Web Tokens (JWT) authentication to Flask applications. It allows you to protect routes and endpoints by requiring valid JWT tokens for access.

Installation:

```bash
pip install Flask-JWT-Extended
```

Usage:

```python
from flask import Flask
from flask_jwt_extended import JWTManager, jwt_required, create_access_token

app = Flask(__name__)
app.config['JWT_SECRET_KEY'] = 'your-secret-key'
jwt = JWTManager(app)

@app.route('/login', methods=['POST'])
def login():
    # Authenticate user
    access_token = create_access_token(identity='username')
    return {'access_token': access_token}

@app.route('/protected', methods=['GET'])
@jwt_required()
def protected():
    return {'message': 'Protected route'}
```

Flask-JWT-Extended provides a simple way to implement token-based authentication in your Flask APIs, ensuring secure access to protected resources.

Flask-SQLAlchemy: Database Integration

Flask-SQLAlchemy is an extension that simplifies database integration in Flask applications by providing a high-level interface to SQLAlchemy, a powerful SQL toolkit and Object-Relational Mapping (ORM) library.

Installation:

```bash
pip install Flask-SQLAlchemy
```

Usage:

```python
from flask import Flask
from flask_sqlalchemy import SQLAlchemy

app = Flask(__name__)
app.config['SQLALCHEMY_DATABASE_URI'] = 'sqlite:///test.db'
db = SQLAlchemy(app)

class User(db.Model):
    id = db.Column(db.Integer, primary_key=True)
    username = db.Column(db.String(80), unique=True, nullable=False)
```

```
    email = db.Column(db.String(120), unique=True, nullable=False)

    def __repr__(self):
        return '<User %r>' % self.username
```

Flask-SQLAlchemy makes it easy to define database models, perform CRUD operations, and manage database connections within your Flask application.

Flask-Cache: Caching

Flask-Cache is an extension that adds caching support to Flask applications, allowing you to cache expensive or frequently accessed data to improve performance and reduce response times.

Installation:

```bash
pip install Flask-Cache
```

Usage:

```python
from flask import Flask
```

```
from flask_cache import Cache

app = Flask(__name__)
cache = Cache(app)

@app.route('/')
@cache.cached(timeout=60)
def hello():
    return 'Hello, World!'
```

With Flask-Cache, you can configure caching strategies, expiration times, and cache backends to optimize the performance of your Flask APIs.

Flask-Testing: Unit Testing

Flask-Testing is an extension that provides utilities and helpers for writing unit tests for Flask applications. It simplifies the process of testing routes, views, and other components of your Flask API.

Installation:

```bash
pip install Flask-Testing
```

Usage:

```python
from flask_testing import TestCase
from myapp import app

class MyTest(TestCase):
    def create_app(self):
        return app

    def test_home(self):
        response = self.client.get('/')
        self.assertEqual(response.status_code, 200)
        self.assertIn(b'Hello, World!', response.data)
```

Flask-Testing allows you to write test cases for your Flask APIs using familiar testing frameworks such as unittest or pytest, ensuring the reliability and correctness of your code.

Flask extensions provide a wide range of functionality to streamline common tasks, enhance functionality, and improve productivity in Flask API development. By leveraging extensions such as Flask-CORS, Flask-JWT-Extended, Flask-SQLAlchemy, Flask-Cache, and Flask-Testing, you can simplify authentication, database integration, caching, testing, and more, making it easier to build robust and scalable Flask APIs. With Flask extensions, you can accelerate development, improve code quality, and deliver high-performance APIs that meet the needs of your users and customers.

Conclusion

In conclusion, Flask API development offers a versatile and powerful platform for building robust and scalable APIs that meet the needs of modern web and mobile applications. By following best practices and leveraging the rich ecosystem of Flask extensions, developers can streamline development, enhance functionality, and deliver high-performance APIs that drive innovation and create value for users and businesses alike.

Throughout this journey, we've explored a myriad of best practices, from RESTful design principles to data serialization, authentication mechanisms, testing strategies, and more. We've delved into the intricacies of Flask extensions like Flask-RESTful, Marshmallow, Flask-JWT-Extended, Flask-SQLAlchemy, and Flask-Cache, discovering how they can supercharge development and streamline common tasks.

With Flask, developers have the flexibility to design APIs that adhere to RESTful principles, ensuring consistency, predictability, and scalability. By structuring endpoints around data resources and versioning APIs effectively, developers can facilitate smooth transitions and backward compatibility, enabling seamless integration and evolution of their APIs over time.

Authentication mechanisms such as token-based authentication with JWT and role-based access control provide granular control over user permissions, ensuring secure access to resources and protecting sensitive data. By implementing authentication with Flask extensions, developers can enforce security best practices and safeguard their APIs against unauthorized access and malicious attacks.

Data handling, validation, and serialization are critical aspects of Flask API development, and extensions like Marshmallow simplify these tasks, enabling effortless data manipulation and transformation. With Marshmallow, developers can define schemas for their data models, validate incoming data, and serialize/deserialize objects with ease, ensuring data integrity and consistency across the API.

Testing is another crucial aspect of Flask API development, and extensions like Flask-Testing provide utilities and helpers for writing comprehensive unit and integration tests. By adopting test-driven development (TDD) practices and leveraging testing frameworks, developers can ensure the reliability and correctness of their code, reducing bugs, and improving overall code quality.

Flask's rich ecosystem of extensions empowers developers to address various use cases and challenges in API development, from authentication and database integration to caching, documentation, and beyond. By selecting and integrating the right extensions for their projects, developers can accelerate development, improve productivity, and deliver APIs that meet the highest standards of performance, security, and usability.

In the ever-evolving landscape of web and mobile development, Flask API development continues to be a leading choice for developers seeking flexibility, simplicity, and scalability. With its lightweight and modular architecture, coupled with a vibrant community and ecosystem of extensions, Flask remains at the forefront of API development, empowering developers to build innovative and impactful applications that shape the future of technology. So, whether you're a seasoned Flask developer or just starting your journey, embrace best practices, harness the power of Flask extensions, and embark on a path of endless possibilities in API development.

Appendix

Glossary of terms

Here are 10 glossary terms related to Flask API development:

1. Flask: A micro web framework written in Python used for building web applications, including APIs. Flask provides simplicity, flexibility, and extensibility for developers.

2. RESTful: Representational State Transfer (REST) is an architectural style for designing networked applications. A RESTful API adheres to REST principles, including statelessness, resource-based URLs, and standard HTTP methods.

3. Endpoint: A specific URL or route in a web API that corresponds to a resource or action. Endpoints define the functionality exposed by the API and are accessed via HTTP requests.

4. Serialization: The process of converting complex data structures, such as objects or dictionaries, into a format suitable for transmission, storage, or display. In Flask API development, serialization is often used to convert Python objects to JSON or XML.

5. Deserialization: The reverse process of serialization, where data in a specific format (e.g., JSON) is converted back into its original data structure (e.g., Python objects).

6. Authentication: The process of verifying the identity of users or clients accessing an API. Authentication mechanisms, such as API keys, tokens, or OAuth, are used to ensure secure access to resources.

7. Authorization: The process of determining whether a user or client has permission to access a specific resource or perform a particular action within an API. Authorization mechanisms, such as role-based access control (RBAC), define user permissions and privileges.

8. ORM (Object-Relational Mapping): A programming technique for converting data between incompatible type systems, such as between objects in object-oriented programming languages and relational databases. Flask-SQLAlchemy is an ORM extension for Flask that simplifies database integration.

9. Middleware: Software components or modules that intercept and process requests and responses in a web application's request/response cycle. Middleware can perform tasks such as authentication, logging, error handling, and caching.

10. Testing: The process of evaluating the behavior, functionality, and performance of a web API through automated tests. Unit tests, integration tests, and end-to-end tests are common types of tests used in Flask API development to ensure the reliability and correctness of the codebase.

Common Flask API Development Pitfalls (and How to Avoid Them!)

Common Flask API development pitfalls can arise from various aspects of the development process, including architecture, design, implementation, testing, and deployment. By understanding these pitfalls and adopting best practices, developers can avoid common mistakes and build robust, scalable, and maintainable Flask APIs. In this article, we'll explore some of the most common pitfalls in Flask API development and provide guidance on how to avoid them.

1. Lack of Proper Error Handling

One of the most common pitfalls in Flask API development is insufficient error handling. Without proper error handling, APIs can expose sensitive information, return generic error messages, or fail to provide adequate feedback to clients.

How to Avoid: Implement comprehensive error handling mechanisms using Flask's error handling features, such as `@app.errorhandler` decorator and custom exception classes. Provide informative error messages, use appropriate HTTP status codes, and handle exceptions gracefully to prevent unexpected behavior.

```python
from flask import Flask, jsonify

app = Flask(__name__)

@app.errorhandler(404)
def not_found_error(error):
    return jsonify({'error': 'Not found'}), 404

if __name__ == '__main__':
    app.run(debug=True)
```

2. Overlooking Input Validation

Failing to validate user input can lead to security vulnerabilities, data integrity issues, and unexpected behavior in Flask APIs. Input validation ensures that data passed to API endpoints meets specified criteria and prevents injection attacks, data corruption, and other security threats.

How to Avoid: Use validation libraries like Marshmallow or Flask-WTF to define schemas and validate request data. Implement input validation logic in API endpoints to sanitize and validate incoming data before processing.

```python
from marshmallow import Schema, fields, ValidationError

class UserSchema(Schema):
    username = fields.Str(required=True)

@app.route('/user', methods=['POST'])
def create_user():
    try:
        data = request.json
        UserSchema().load(data)
        # Process user creation logic
        return jsonify({'message': 'User created successfully'})
    except ValidationError as e:
        return jsonify({'error': e.messages}), 400
```

3. Inefficient Database Access

Inefficient database access can lead to performance bottlenecks, slow response times, and poor scalability in Flask APIs. Inadequate query optimization, lack of indexing, and unnecessary database calls can degrade API performance and impact user experience.

How to Avoid: Optimize database queries by using SQLAlchemy's query optimization techniques, indexing relevant columns, and minimizing the number of database calls. Use caching mechanisms to reduce database load and improve response times for frequently accessed data.

```python
from flask_sqlalchemy import SQLAlchemy

app = Flask(__name__)
db = SQLAlchemy(app)

class User(db.Model):
    id = db.Column(db.Integer, primary_key=True)
    username = db.Column(db.String(50), unique=True, nullable=False)

@app.route('/users')
def get_users():
    users = User.query.all()  # Inefficient query
    return jsonify([user.username for user in users])
```

4. Neglecting Authentication and Authorization

Ignoring authentication and authorization mechanisms can expose APIs to security vulnerabilities, unauthorized access, and data breaches. Without proper authentication and authorization controls, APIs are susceptible to brute-force attacks, data leaks, and unauthorized access to sensitive resources.

How to Avoid: Implement robust authentication mechanisms, such as JWT tokens or OAuth, to verify the identity of clients and users accessing the API. Use role-based access control (RBAC) or permissions systems to enforce authorization policies and restrict access to authorized users only.

```python
from flask_jwt_extended import JWTManager, jwt_required, create_access_token

app = Flask(__name__)
app.config['JWT_SECRET_KEY'] = 'your-secret-key'
jwt = JWTManager(app)

@app.route('/login', methods=['POST'])
def login():
    # Authenticate user
    access_token = create_access_token(identity='username')
    return {'access_token': access_token}

@app.route('/protected', methods=['GET'])
```

```
@jwt_required()
def protected():
    return {'message': 'Protected route'}
```

5. Neglecting Testing

Neglecting testing can result in unstable, unreliable APIs that are prone to bugs, regressions, and unexpected behavior. Without proper testing, developers may overlook edge cases, fail to validate functionality, and introduce errors that go unnoticed until they cause production issues.

How to Avoid: Adopt a comprehensive testing strategy that includes unit tests, integration tests, and end-to-end tests for API endpoints, business logic, and edge cases. Use testing frameworks like pytest or Flask-Testing to automate testing and ensure the reliability and correctness of the API.

```python
import pytest
from myapp import app

@pytest.fixture
def client():
    app.config['TESTING'] = True
```

```
    with app.test_client() as client:
        yield client

def test_hello(client):
    response = client.get('/')
    assert response.status_code == 200
    assert b'Hello, World!' in response.data
```

By avoiding these common pitfalls and following best practices in Flask API development, developers can build robust, secure, and scalable APIs that meet the needs of modern web and mobile applications. Prioritizing error handling, input validation, database optimization, authentication, authorization, and testing ensures the reliability, security, and performance of Flask APIs, ultimately leading to a better user experience and higher developer satisfaction. With careful planning, attention to detail, and adherence to best practices, Flask developers can navigate the challenges of API development and deliver high-quality solutions that stand the test of time.

www.ingramcontent.com/pod-product-compliance
Lightning Source LLC
Chambersburg PA
CBHW031614210526
45464CB00004B/1581